5-7

CHICAGO PUBLIC LIBRARY

R00515 01025

COMPUTERS IN THE CURRICULUM SERIES
Howard Budin and Diane S. Kendall, Editors

Using Computers in the Social Studies
Howard Budin, Diane S. Kendall, and James Lengel

Using Computers in the Teaching of Reading
Dorothy S. Strickland, Shelley Weoner, and Joan Feeley

Ref.

LB
1584
.B76
1986

Budin, Howard, 1946–

Using computers in
the social studies

Chicago Public Library

C
P L

REFERENCE

Form 178 rev. 1-94

SOCIAL SCIENCES & HISTORY DIVISION

ION

EDUCATION & PHILOSOPHY

© THE BAKER & TAYLOR CO.

Using Computers in the Social Studies

Howard Budin
Diane S. Kendall
James Lengel

REFERENCE USE ONLY

TEACHERS COLLEGE PRESS

Teachers College, Columbia University
New York and London

SOCIAL SCIENCE & HISTORY DIVISION
EDUCATION & PHILOSOPHY SECTION

REF
LB
1584
.B76
1986

515 0/025

Published by Teachers College Press, 1234 Amsterdam Avenue,
New York, N.Y. 10027

© 1986 by Teachers College, Columbia University
All rights reserved. No part of this publication may be reproduced
or transmitted in any form or by any means, electronic or mechanical,
including photocopy, or any information storage and retrieval system,
without permission from the publisher.

Library of Congress Cataloging in Publication Data

Budin, Howard, 1946–
   Using computers in the social studies.

   (Computers in the curriculum series)
   Includes index.
   1. Social sciences—Computer-assisted instruction.
   2. Social sciences—Study and teaching (Elementary)
   3. Social sciences—Study and teaching (Secondary)
   I. Kendall, Diane S., 1952–   . II. Lengel, James,
   1949–   . III. Title. IV. Series.
   LB1584.B76   1986   372.3'5044   85-27779
   ISBN 0-8077-2781-4 (pbk.)

Manufactured in the United States of America

91 90 89 88 87 86   1 2 3 4 5 6

Contents

SOCIAL SCIENCE & HISTORY DIVISION
EDUCATION & PHILOSOPHY SECTION

Preface

Math and science teachers, beware! Those computers sitting in your classrooms are soon going to be just as much in demand in the classrooms of your social studies colleagues. Social studies teachers are rapidly finding out what a useful tool the computer can be and are putting it and other technologies to work in their classrooms.

And that is what this book is all about: how to bring the computer into the social studies classroom. Although the full dynamic potential of the computer in the social studies classroom may not be realized until a few more years have passed, there is much going on in the field already. Over the last three or four years, we have put together workshops and a course for teachers that cover many of these developments. The structure of this book is a result of the very practical approach we have taken in trying to cover the spectrum of how the computer can, and may in the future, affect social studies instruction.

This book was not designed as an exhaustive resource on the subject. That would be a foolhardy, if not impossible, task in a field that is undergoing rapid change. Instead, our goal has been to provide a basic introduction to the use of computers in social studies teaching and to answer teachers' questions. For example, you may ask, Why use computers at all? Do they really have something of value to contribute, or are they just part of a fashionable trend? What can you do in the classroom with computers that you couldn't do without them? What are some specific applications? What kind of computer equipment and instructional materials are available? What other computer-related technologies might be helpful in teaching social studies? What are some of the issues that the use of computers and other technology may create for society, and how can you teach about them in your classroom?

We have also provided some basic information about how computers work, what types are available, other computer-related technologies, and the limitations of each. We believe that you don't have to know anything about computers in order to read and understand this book.

We hope that you will find this approach useful. The computer is a new tool that, properly handled, can help make the social studies classroom a much more exciting place for students and teachers alike. All that it takes to get started is a little background information.

Using Computers
in the Social Studies

□ 1 □
New Tools for Social Studies Education

The scenarios that follow may sound like glimpses of the future. But all of them can happen today.

• Assigned to play the role of a journalist covering Woodrow Wilson's conduct of the negotiations for the United States at the Versailles peace conference, Kathy found herself staying late at school each day to study and record the progress of the conference on her school's "Versailles Simulation," a computer-managed simulation of the diplomatic maneuvering that took place before the signing of the Treaty of Versailles. Kathy used the word processing capabilities of the school's computer to compose and "file" reports of the arguments and compromises hammered out at the daily treaty sessions. The computer program also contained extensive information on and pertinent literature from the World War I era that Kathy and other students could access and use as they made their way through the simulation.

• The first-period history class had trouble understanding the concept of "search and seizure" as written into the Fifth Amendment to the Constitution and as modified in the 200 years since ratification. So the teacher called up three short dramatic segments from a computerized videodisk: one illustrating a search by British agents using "writs of assistance," another simulating the classic case study of the police search of Dolly Mapp's apartment, and a third showing a present-day "stop-and-frisk" situation. Comparison of these three,

1

using stop action and careful class discussions, allowed the students to grasp the issues at hand. The second-period class viewed a dramatization of Clarence Earl Gideon's trial (taken from the movie *Gideon's Trumpet,* starring Henry Fonda), available on the same videodisk.

  • Having been assigned the role of prosecutors, it was John's team's turn to use the computer. The team had just met and decided to interview two more witnesses before going to trial. The witnesses' depositions were on file, deep in the confines of the computer's memory. The prosecution team accessed them as part of the "Mock Trial" program. When both defense and prosecution were finally ready to start, the computer managed the courtroom proceedings and rendered a verdict based on the evidence presented to it by both teams during the trial.

  • It was the evening of the annual city meeting in which the voters would make decisions on city matters, and the meeting was being broadcast on the local television station. Two of the voters, Bob and Marilyn, sat at home in front of their television set, with the teletext console keyboard on the couch between them. They had just watched an informed debate on a proposed new zoning regulation and were now discussing it. After five minutes, the meeting moderator told everyone it was time to vote. By typing "yes" into the console, Marilyn cast a vote in favor of the measure. Bob, turning so Marilyn couldn't see, typed in "no." Within a few moments, citywide voting totals appeared on the television screen.

  • Treetop Teachers College was quiet this late in the evening. Professor Mark Stella was seated at the small computer, alternately typing on the keyboard and eyeing the screen. He was perusing the responses he had received to his latest query of the Social Studies Network (SSN) concerning new materials on the teaching of ancient Chinese history to use in his social studies methods course. To his delight, he found three bibliographic references and a computer program on the topic, the last of which he "downloaded" (or transferred) into his computer's memory. At the end of the list of information from SSN, he came across an urgent bulletin from the National Council for the Social Studies asking viewers to write their congressional representatives about a new bill concerning federal funding for libraries.

• Annie was preparing her research paper on antitrust law. She had found lots of material on the Sugar Trust and on Standard Oil cases, but there wasn't much in the school library on the recent IBM, AT&T, or Cereal Trust cases. So the librarian showed her how to use the school's computer to access WESTLAW, a computer program containing a data base (a large amount of electronically stored data) on important legal cases. Here Annie found summaries of recent court decisions on two of the three cases. With a sigh of relief, she ripped the printout from the printer and went off to finish writing her paper.

• As part of its study of the various geographic regions of the United States, the fourth-grade class at Central Elementary School had assembled hundreds of bits of information about the various states, entering them into a data-base program on the computer in the back of the room. After they had finished entering this data base into the computer, they could call up and review various relationships among the states and regions: In which region was the annual rainfall greatest? Where was it least? Do the rainfall figures have any connection with the agricultural products in each region? All of these explorations were done from the keyboard, using the data that the students themselves had assembled.

• Teams of eighth-grade students were enjoying piloting sailing ships westward across an unknown ocean, navigating by the stars (the computer screen becomes, among other things, the night sky), keeping track of their longitude and latitude, then making decisions on how long and in which direction to sail. Each team used the computer in turn, hoping to find the uncharted new continent before their provisions gave out.

• Oscar had trouble understanding how to use coordinates to locate places on a map. Diane needed some help understanding how the Bill of Rights could be applied to present-day situations. So both Oscar and Diane were spending their fifth-period study hall in the library, each working with the computer disk that their social studies teacher had assigned them to use. Oscar was tracing his way around the village of Littleton, which was represented on the computer screen, complete with coordinate markings. Diane's computer was tutoring her by guiding her through a set of case studies concerning citizens' rights that are protected by the Bill of Rights, and relevant situations from recent newspaper stories.

All of these situations involve new electronic technologies. Each also involves, very directly, social studies education.

The students controlling the Versailles Treaty simulation are practicing and learning participation skills and are gaining a better understanding of the nature of world politics.

By using a videodisk, the social studies teacher is bringing into the classroom a variety of outside resources from past and present to help illustrate the social studies concepts (the search-and-seizure issue) that she is teaching.

In the mock trial conducted on the computer, students are learning the procedures of the justice system and practicing their reasoning and participation skills.

Bob and Marilyn are taking part in an "electronic town meeting" that illustrates how technology might enable us to return to a more participatory direct democracy.

Up-to-date resources (including bibliographic references, computer software, and innovative lesson plans) for training teachers in social studies are made immediately available to Professor Stella, even though he is at a small college, through an easy-to-use electronic network.

Annie is able to perform advanced legal research from her school library by using another computer-based network.

The data base assembled by the fourth-grade class at Central Elementary School allows them to quickly test hypotheses about the nature of various regions of the United States. Such a data base could easily be expanded to compare similar regions from around the world. The charts and graphs constructed by the computer, using the children's data, appears in the same formal format as the information in the student's textbooks and other references. This reinforces the children's positive feelings about their work.

By using the computer to simulate the problems of navigating an unknown ocean, students begin to empathize with early explorers.

Oscar and Diane are able to receive individual independent remedial help to supplement their classwork by using the computer.

Possibly these examples, at first glance, may seem farfetched, since some of them have not yet been widely implemented in social studies classrooms. But every one of them is possible with present-day technology; most of them have actually taken place in various classrooms and homes all over the United States already.

Contribution of Computers to the Social Studies

As these glimpses of computers in action illustrate, the relationship of social studies to computers is limited only by our imaginations. Technical wizardry is rapidly catching up with efforts to enliven and enrich social studies teaching. In the meantime, social studies educators must acquire some basic facts about how to use what already is available to them, as well as learn about "what might be," in order to demand more in the future.

It is imperative in this process, though, for educators to gain perspective on what computers are really offering the social studies. It will be a long time in the future, if ever, that the computer will take the place of the social studies teacher. At present the computer cannot replace the uncanny ability and wit of a teacher who throws in amusing and appropriate historical anecdotes (and gossip) at just the right moment of a lecture or a discussion, nor can it communicate heartfelt feelings about people, places, and events in history as related by someone who truly loves the subject. Because of its current technical limitations, the computer also cannot mimic the devil's advocate approach to the issue of slavery, or some other controversy, that a teacher can use to help students see both sides of an issue.

With our help, computers can reflect many of the human qualities of a master teacher: enthusiasm, knowledge, discipline, and the gift of encouraging others. This should be the ultimate goal of those developing computer materials. The one-on-one contact between teachers and students, however, should not, and will not be replaced by the machine.

In addition to depending on the teacher, social studies education also depends on the use of great volumes of printed materials and artifacts that can be examined in the classroom. Because of its limited memory capacity, the computer, even in its most advanced stages, probably will not, at least in our lifetimes, replace the use of books. The use of primary and secondary resource materials and artifacts now used to help bring alive the joys and sorrows, and the problems and perplexities, of individuals and groups from different times and places will continue to play an important role in the social studies classroom.

There are many ways that the computer can enhance the methods already being used by social studies teachers. Although they cannot replace books, computer networks of libraries are now helping students doing research projects to locate bibliographic references and other resources that otherwise might have gone unnoticed. Simulations, drill-and-practice exercises, remediation lessons, and demonstrations are only a few of the other extensions of methods already in practice that can be enhanced by the interactive memory capabilities of computers. (All of these applications will be described in detail later in this book.) We need to remember, however, that although some things can be done better on the computer, others cannot. We are only beginning to experiment with how the computer can help us. For now and in the future, the computer offers the social studies teacher a new tool or resource: no more, no less.

A Slow Start

Until recently, many social studies educators have not had the opportunity to make use of computers or have been hesitant about getting started. Educational publishers and houses that specialize in producing educational computer programs (software publishers) are just beginning to develop materials or applications for computers at all levels of social studies education. Although many significant individual pioneering efforts are being made in the field, they are just beginning to be recognized (see Chapter 2). In the meantime, the network of people interested in social studies computer applications is growing rapidly, and the amount of materials directly related to the field triples each year.

Lack of money is perhaps the number one reason cited to explain why more progress has not been made in linking social studies and computers in the public school system. School administrators, pushed to bring computers into their school districts, often do not have enough funds to provide them for all subject areas or grade levels in their schools. They, along with the general public, assume that the best places to install their few computers are in their math and science classrooms, where computers seem to have the most obvious applications. Unfortunately, the computers often become entangled in the usual departmental squabbles and jealousies, and social studies teachers may end up with little or no exposure or access to computers.

For many social studies teachers, this situation suits them just fine. Perhaps the strongest reason why computers and social studies have not forged a stronger link is probably social studies teachers themselves. Many went into social studies education partly in an effort to get away from anything quantitative. Anything that remotely reminds them of mathematics is anathema. Some have confided that they are terrified that they might touch the wrong button on a computer and cause it to explode. When they hear that it often takes 1,000 hours for a nonmathematical person to write the codes that make up a computer program, they tune out anything more that can be said about the wonders of the computer age — not realizing that one can acquire computer literacy without learning how to program a computer.

Others, concerned about the autonomy of the individual in society, have a basic distrust of machines that might eliminate the human element in making decisions or reasoning out problems. They often claim, despite growing evidence to the contrary, that computers are just another fad that will pass.

Until recently, few social studies teachers were offered the kind of computer training that focused on their needs and concerns. Lately there has been great emphasis on making computers more accessible to all kinds of people and less the exclusive domain of mathematical geniuses. As more computers enter the home market and the realm of top business executives (many of whom have neither the time nor the inclination to become computer experts), computers are becoming more accessible to even the most timid of computer users — even social studies teachers.

Publications for the social studies classroom teacher have also been slow to include practical articles on how to get started with computers. This trend is being reversed. The National Council for the Social Studies, the largest organization of social studies teachers, has begun to reserve time at its regional conferences for teachers to be exposed to commercial publishers and others who are developing computer-based materials. The council's journal, *Social Education*, now includes a monthly article on what is new in the computer field and in other related technologies such as videodisks and cable networks. Other major articles have appeared, and an entire issue has been devoted to the computer. Recently other educational journals and computer-oriented magazines for teachers have begun to include articles on how to use computers in the social studies classroom. This movement seems to be growing rapidly as more social studies teachers take the plunge.

As for the other concerns of some social studies teachers — such as the fear that computers — those purely logical machines without social consciences — are going to take over the world: Only time will tell. There is a case to be made, though, for exploring the link between social studies and computers in the face of the shrinking amount of classroom time being devoted to social studies at all levels of elementary and secondary education. As computers stimulate experimentation and funding in other content areas, it would be foolhardy not to at least conduct a few experiments of our own. As threatening as technology may sometimes seem, social studies education cannot afford to be left behind.

The State of Social Studies Software

Despite optimistic predictions for the future, there is one other sad reality for social studies teachers. Until recently, many of the commercially available computer materials for social studies have been of the drill-and-practice kind (for example, KNOW THE STATES), with limited or no tutorial introductions. Other materials have not fit easily into standard curriculum areas. Although there are some notable exceptions, many of the materials now available are only glorified, computerized versions of printed workbooks that do not take advantage of the graphic capacity of the computer or its ability to interact with the student.

An additional problem is that many of these programs can serve only one student at a time. In other words, if only one computer is available for a class of 30 students, then only one student can use the computer, while the other 29 have to be kept at other tasks. Some programs are designed for use by teams of students, but these are presently in the minority. If only a few computers are available, classroom management can become a major obstacle. (How to resolve this problem is discussed in the appropriate applications sections in Chapter 2.)

This lack of variety, quality, and flexibility in the software materials (that is, computer programs) now available for social studies can be explained by exploring who produced them. Many of these early programs were produced by programmers with little or no expertise in education, much less in social studies. This lack of expertise also affects most of the materials produced for other content areas. Only recently have publishers begun to recognize this problem.

To create good materials, it is necessary to form a team consisting of a programmer who knows how to program, a content specialist to advise on the accuracy of the material, and an instructional designer. The job of the instructional designer is to make sure that the capabilities of the computer are put to maximum use. For example, computer programs should be interactive; in other words, there should be give-and-take between the student and machine. The student should not just be reading material off the screen that could be introduced in a book or other printed form. So far, much of the computer programming that has been developed for all the content areas has tapped only a small part of the capability of the computer. As teachers (and their students) are coming to find out, many of the drill-and-practice or reading comprehension programs that are now commercially available are not very difficult to produce. The growing sophistication of computer users has already created a demand for more complicated materials for all content areas.

The consequences of this new wave of computer materials may have interesting implications for the social studies. The notion that math and science are the most obvious applications for computers may disappear. The broad social studies curriculum — which in most states includes a serving of world geography and cultures, world history, American history, and a dash of community and state history — offers a smorgasbord of subjects for publishers to get together, garnished with a variety of methods used to teach content and large concepts. Simulations of the problems of different periods of history, of contacts between cultures, and of decision-making processes will be added to the library of available software materials for social studies. Tutorials and drill-and-practice exercises that teach basic skills such as mapping, charting, and graphing will enhance much of what is now done solely with static print materials. Computer programs containing data bases of dates, facts, statistics, and other general information will bring primary materials and raw data to the fingertips of social studies students anxious to try out hypotheses or to prove conclusions. Lectures and discussions will be enlivened by graphic materials generated by the computer.

With some training, this new flood of materials should help to make more social studies teachers comfortable with the new tools available to them, especially those materials that enhance the methods that teachers are already using. Again, the computer is only one more tool available for use by the social studies teacher. It will not create a new social studies curriculum. It may reshape how things are taught, but will not change what is traditionally taught.

Coping with Computers

Computers will change the social studies curriculum, however, in other less direct ways. As we move rapidly toward the twenty-first century, both social studies educators and their students have to be prepared for some of the changes and issues of living in a highly technological age. Statistics from the U.S. Department of Labor indicate that by 1990, 75 percent of all jobs will require some interaction with computers. In the late 1980s and early 1990s, 685,000 new jobs and 250,000 "replacement" jobs directly involving computer operations are expected to develop.

What are all those people going to be doing with those computers? How will this technological revolution affect us socially, politically, economically, militarily, and culturally? Do more computers and computer users mean less privacy for the individual? How have other people, at other times and in other places, coped with technological advances? Do their responses have any lessons for us?

These are only some of the questions that are bound to begin to invade the social studies classroom. Of course, educators in other disciplines will also be discussing these and other issues, but much of the responsibility for helping students explore these topics is going to rest with social studies teachers. Education departments in some states have been discussing ways of responding to this challenge by adding a "History of Technology" component to their World History curriculum. This seems like only a partial solution. Social studies teachers are going to have to develop a new awareness of how to bring many of these issues into the social studies curriculum as a whole. For example, discussion of equal rights might now have to include a segment on whether equal access to technology by the aged, women, minorities, and a broad range of socio-economic groups also has to be guaranteed if the idea of equality for all is to survive. Direct democracy by computer voting at home must also be discussed. Should we take advantage of the opportunity for all citizens to vote quickly and directly on issues such as taxes or military police actions in other nations by U.S. forces? Or can too many cooks spoil the broth?

In Chapter 4, a range of these issues will be discussed in more detail, with suggestions about how and where many of these topics might be discussed in the curriculum. Social studies educators have to become aware that bringing the computer or other technology into the classroom does not end when we turn the machine off. A whole new can of worms is being opened up.

Getting Started

How should social studies educators go about introducing computers into their classrooms? At Teachers College, at Columbia University, one of the workshop series offered by the Computering in Education Program is called "What to Do Until the Computer Arrives." The content of the workshop is not necessarily relevant to social studies, but the title is. Certainly in all levels of the curriculum, discussions of issues relating to changes occurring in people's daily lives as a result of high technology should be included immediately in day-to-day classroom activity. When you start to look for information to help you begin your discussions of these issues, you will probably be amazed how much appears daily or weekly in the media. Start a clipping file on some of the issues that come up in your classroom. Enlist your students' help by having them keep media logs on particular issues.

Next, get comfortable with a computer. The next section of this chapter gives a bare-bones outline of what you need to know about computers in general in order to get started. Get someone who has had some computer exposure to help you get acquainted — a colleague, a friend, or even a student. Students love to show off what they have learned about computers and probably will take the role reversal of becoming the teacher very seriously. Hold on to your ego, and join in.

Next, you should try previewing some of the computer materials discussed in Chapter 2 and try some of them out in your classroom. Chapter 2 also discusses some evaluation procedures, but you should make up your own: After all, you know your students better than anyone else does.

Remember that the computer is only one more tool or resource available to the teacher, and don't expect too much too fast. As you become more comfortable with your and your students' ability to handle the computer, expand your use of it. Find out what computer resources for doing research are available through your library. Have students who enjoy working with computers help you to create your own materials. Create options in your assignments that allow students to use computers by building their own simulation models or to collect and analyze their own data or raw data collected by others.

All of these methods are only extensions of many of the things that you are probably doing already. The difference is that you are giving your students the opportunity to work with the tools of tomorrow, just as the social scientist uses them in the real world of today. Computers linked to the social studies curriculum should allow teachers to give their students new, but potentially even more appropriate experiences, within the traditional education system.

☐   THE COMPUTER AS A SOCIAL STUDIES TOOL   ☐

To be really comfortable with a computer and its capabilities, it is wise to understand a bit about how one works. The computer is an information processor, and as such it is an ideal tool for the social studies student and teacher. Sifting through historical data, making and reading maps, and simulating events are a few of the many social studies tasks that require using large amounts of information, and many computer programs have been developed to handle these tasks. Additional ways of processing information — word processing, filing, statistical analysis, and data communications — were not developed specifically for social studies but have numerous applications.

To use a computer, it is not necessary to be an expert in electronics or programming. Putting a disk (which contains preprogrammed information) into a disk drive (or reader), turning the machine on, and following some printed instructions are usually sufficient. A knowledge of the basic concepts of computer operation, however, can be useful to anyone who comes into contact with computers, and especially to teachers using this technology with students. Understanding how the parts of a computer system interact with computer programs can demystify computer operation, make you feel more comfortable, and give you confidence in using them.

This section presents an overview of how the computer processes information. It describes the function of the parts of a computer system, explains how programs tell the computer what to do, and discusses what kind of tasks a computer can or cannot do. The intention is for you to get a sense of the power, but also the limitations, of using computer technology.

Hardware

Computers are best described as systems: They are made up of a number of interconnected components. The physical parts of the system are called the hardware, and any computer system must have at least four parts: an input component; an output component; a Central Processing Unit (CPU), and a memory or storage component. Let's consider the hardware for each of these parts in turn.

Input. Computer input is the information that is put into a computer. The most common way to "input" information is by pushing buttons or keys. Most computers come with keyboards. The cash machine at your bank and some electronic toys have keypads with just a few keys to press. Other input devices common in video games are game paddles or a joystick that you use to tell the computer which way to move some figure on the screen. A third kind of input is in the form of magnetized signals on a tape or disk. For example, to use a bank cash machine, you must insert your card and input your security code by pushing the correct keys. The computer reads, or gets input from, the magnetized strip on the back of the card: This is the information it uses to check whether your code is correct. Magnetic tapes and disks can also be used to input information that the computer needs in order to operate.

Output. Computer output is the opposite of input: information sent out from the computer to the user. The two most common output devices are screens and printers. Think again of how you use a bank card. Messages appear on a little screen and can also be printed out for you on paper: this is called a hard copy. Another kind of output is sound: music or speech or other noises, produced by a speaker, that typically emanate from video games. Speech synthesizers can be connected to some computers that simulate human speech.

Central Processing Unit. The CPU is sometimes called the "brain" of the computer; it directs all of the computer's operations. Specifically, it does three kinds of jobs: It handles all the input and output, does arithmetic, and compares one piece of data with another. These are all of the functions that a computer uses to do any task. The CPU needs a *program*, or a piece of *software*, however, to instruct it step-by-step. When we discuss software later in this chapter, we will see how a task can be broken down into the three functions that a CPU is made to perform. The CPU is located inside the main computer unit, on one or more chips — integrated circuits of miniaturized electronic wiring.

Memory. There are two kinds of memory components: the main computer memory, consisting of tiny circuits, which resides inside the main computer unit near the CPU; and secondary storage, which is attached to a computer in the form of a tape recorder or disk drive. Secondary storage is optional, but it is necessary if you want to save any information permanently, since most information stored in the main memory is erased when the computer is turned off or when other information is put into it.

Suppose you have a disk with various programs stored on it. To run one of the programs, you use a command that tells the CPU to transfer a copy of that program from the disk to the main memory. When you are through with that program and want to see another, you do the same thing: make a copy from the disk to main memory. This erases the first program from the main memory, but it does not affect either program on the disk; you only made copies from the disk and put them into the computer memory one at a time.

These four elements make up a computer system, as you can see illustrated in Figure 1.1. Notice that the arrows going into the computer processing unit indicate input, and those pointing out indicate output. Secondary storage can be used either for input or output. In the situation described in the preceding paragraph, a disk drive was used for input: Programs were transferred into the computer. The opposite can also be done: A program in the computer can be saved (or "output") onto a disk or tape. Notice also that the CPU and the main computer memory are situated inside the computer unit and that the other parts are wired to it in one way or another.

Figure 1.1. *A Computer System.*

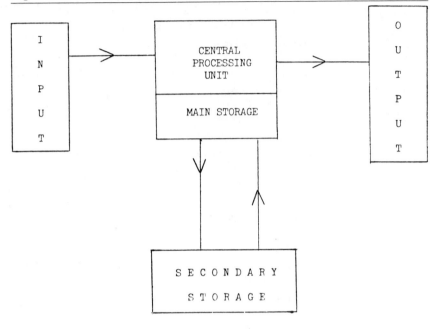

Microcomputers, Mainframes, and Networking

Microcomputers, made possible by advances in miniaturizing electronic circuits, have been on the market for only about ten years, during which time they have proliferated in homes and schools and undergone many variations. A microcomputer is a small, portable computer, and all of the parts of the system are physically present when you use it. Input is usually via a keyboard, which may either be part of the main computer unit or detachable. Output typically comes through a monitor, or screen device, which can be built into the unit or a separate device connected to it. A printer may also be connected, or interfaced, with the computer for output. The main computer memory and the CPU are located inside the main unit, and the secondary storage component is interfaced with it.

A mainframe computer usually has much more storage capability than a microcomputer, and this allows more than one person to use it at the same time. The parts of a mainframe computer are not all necessarily together in one place. The CPU and the main and secondary storage are in one place, but the input/output devices, called *terminals,* can be very widely scattered. Think once more of the bank machine. The machine in front of which you stand is not the whole computer: It is a terminal (input and output) connected to the computer by wires or telephone lines. Many people are probably using the computer at the same time — this is called time sharing — at different bank machines. Bank employees also access the same mainframe on their terminals inside the bank.

The situation of many terminals all accessing the same mainframe is an example of networking. Two or more mainframes can also be networked to each other. An important trend these days is to use microcomputers as parts of networks also: the microcomputer can be made to act as a terminal to a mainframe computer, or one microcomputer can be connected to another. The purpose of all this networking is communication among computer users, and it is usually done through the telephone lines. Data, or information, from the computer or terminal is translated into acoustical signals with a device known as a *modem* and sent through the telephone lines to the other end, where another modem translates the signal back to the digital form that the computer needs.

Communication through computers can take many forms. By networking, users can send mail or information to each other. Individuals can subscribe to services on mainframes that provide updated news, sports reports, and other information. There are "bulletin board" services on which users can leave messages for others to read. These and other applications, and the issues they raise, will be discussed later in the book.

Software

Computer programs, or software, are series of instructions that tell the computer, step-by-step, what tasks to perform. They are written not in English but in specially developed languages, such as BASIC, Pascal, and FORTRAN, that can be translated so that the computer's CPU can process them. Each of these languages consists of a relatively small number of command words — small in comparison to natural languages, that is. One command might tell the computer to get input, another to give output, a third to add two numbers, and a fourth to compare two pieces of data to see if they are the same.

To illustrate how software works, let's take a simple example of a classroom activity and reformulate it for computer use. We won't actually code it in a programming language, but we will break it into steps in the way a programmer might while getting ready to code it. Here is the situation: A history teacher is giving a quiz with ten questions. She wants to keep track of the right answers so that she can tell each student what percentage he or she got correct.

First, let's break this task down into smaller and more precise units, still describing it in plain English:

Repeat 10 times:
    1. Ask a question.
    2. Get an answer.
    3. Evaluate the answer.
        a. If the answer is correct, then do 2 things:
            (1) Praise the student, and
            (2) Add 1 to the number correct.
        b. If the answer is not correct, then tell the correct answer.
Divide the number correct by 10, and
Tell the student the percentage.

This formulation is probably a more precise one than you would conceive of by yourself if you were giving a quiz, but it is not precise enough for a computer, which, after all, cannot understand English. Before actually writing this problem in a programming language, a programmer might plan it more exactly in the form of a flowchart.

Figure 1.2 shows such a flowchart for the above steps. Note that in a flowchart, the various kinds of operations involved are represented by certain geometrical shapes. In this example we use four shapes:

1. The *oval* is the symbol for the beginning and the end of the chart.
2. *Parallelograms* indicate all input and output operations. There are five parallelograms in the chart, and four of them represent output: Ask a question; Congratulate the student; Give the right answer; and Tell student the percentage correct. They are output because they are messages that go out from the computer to the student. Only one parallelogram is input: Get answer. In this step the computer will stop and wait for the student to input the answer, probably by typing it.
3. *Rectangles* stand for internal operations that the computer performs. In our chart there are three such operations, all arithmetical: Set number correct to 0; Add 1 to the number correct; and Divide number correct by 10.
4. *Diamonds* are decision points. A computer can make true–false type decisions. It can evaluate, Is the answer right? If so, the program will branch in the YES direction; if not, the branching will be in the NO direction. A second decision point comes a little later: Asked 10 questions yet? If true, follow the YES path, and if false, follow the NO path.

Figure 1.2. *Flowchart for a Ten-question Test.*

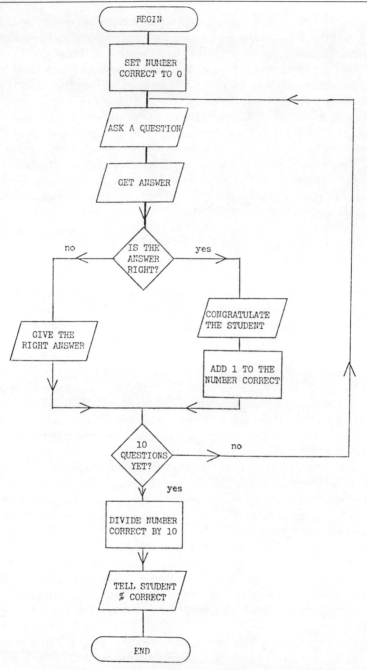

To read a flowchart, simply follow the instructions one by one, starting from the BEGIN oval. Lines connect the instructions, and in case there is more than one way to go, follow the direction of the arrow. The first step in our chart tells the computer to set the number correct to 0. Since computers keep careful counts, we need to make sure that at the beginning of the program there are no correct answers counted.

From this point on, the steps in the chart correspond to our steps written out above. We ask a question and get the answer, then evaluate whether it is correct or not. If it is, we follow the YES path, congratulate the student, and add 1 to the number correct. If not, we simply give the correct answer. In both cases, we move on to the next diamond and decide whether we have asked 10 questions yet. If not, we go back to the "Ask a question" parallelogram. If 10 questions have been asked, we proceed downward, figure out the percentage correct, and announce it.

Computer Decisions

A flowchart is not a computer language, but it does represent fairly closely the commands you would see in a program. The flowchart is not as detailed as a program would be. In fact, several key points are left out of ours. For instance, how does the computer know how to evaluate whether the answer is correct or not? Furthermore, how does it even know what question to ask or what the correct answer should be? All of this information would have to be stored inside the computer, probably in a file of data put on the disk by the programmer. This data file would contain each question and each correct answer. The flowchart could be refined by showing that before the computer asks the question, it must go to that file and get the information about it.

The key point being made here is that computers do only what someone programs them to do. They "know" nothing by themselves; they have no inherent values; and they make decisions only as instructed by a program. These days we hear a lot about "intelligent" programs, terminals, and computers. The more complex the program, the more decision points are put into it, and the more intelligent the program seems. The field of artificial intelligence is very busy trying to discover ways to simulate what we call intelligence, and it is coming up with interesting results. But it is important to remember that by itself a computer is nothing but some electrical wiring ready to interpret and execute detailed instructions given to it.

How, then, do computers make decisions? Take the first diamond decision point in our flowchart: Is the answer correct? To evaluate this, the computer must compare two pieces of data. Remember, we said above that the computer was instructed to get a question and an answer from the data file on a disk. Suppose the question was "What is the capital of Ohio?" and the answer stored on the disk was "Columbus." The computer stores the word "Columbus" in its memory and outputs the question on the screen. Then it gets input from the student, who types in the answer via the keyboard. This input is also stored in the computer's memory. When the computer gets to the decision point, it compares the two pieces of data in its memory; the answer from the file and the input from the keyboard. (Comparing data, you will recall, is one of the functions of the Central Processing Unit.) If the two match exactly, character for character, the computer takes the YES path on the chart. If they are at all different, it takes the NO path.

We have explained this evaluation process in such detail to give you a sense of how much is involved in instructing computers to make decisions. You can also get a sense of some of the difficulties involved. Suppose you would like the student to have a choice of correct answers. Or suppose you don't care whether the answer that is input is typed slightly incorrectly. More programming would be needed to take care of each of these contingencies: The computer has to be told everything.

Understanding something about this process should make you appreciate a program's limitations. Very often, when running a program you will come up against something that it will not do, or you may think the program's method of doing something is stupid. Just remember that the program does exactly what it was programmed to do, no more and no less. Giving you more options while running it means putting more into the program.

On the other hand, the power and speed of operation of modern computers should be appreciated. Microcomputers can now store hundreds of thousands of characters of data in their main memories, and millions of characters in a disk drive. They can operate at speeds of millions of cycles per second. Think of the scenarios presented at the beginning of this chapter. Computers can access and search through remote data bases, scan 54,000 frames on a videodisk to find a picture, evaluate factors simulating an ocean voyage — all in seconds. And the power of the computer is steadily growing — the power, that is, to follow directions quickly and to store large amounts of information.

This book will not teach you to program computers. This skill can take a long time to learn well, but to use a computer there is no need to be able to program it. All of our scenarios show people using applications of the computer; none of them needed to know anything about how the computer was doing what it did. In this section we have tried to give you an idea of what computers can and cannot do, how they operate by "making decisions"—comparing one piece of stored data with another—and how programmers must instruct them at every step.

Knowing these things will help you evaluate and use programs. We turn now to look at the various specific applications of the computer in the social studies.

□ 2 □
Applying the Computer

The microcomputers that we use in classrooms are called general-purpose computers because they can do a variety of tasks, depending on what software you are running. One minute your computer can be a word processor, and the next you can turn it into a statistical analyzer or a simulation-running machine. In this chapter we discuss the large collection of software materials now available that enables your computer to do such different jobs.

Basic Computer Applications

Each section of this chapter describes a distinct use of the computer in the social studies classroom. The individual sections, however, can be grouped into a few overall categories of computer use. One of the main ways that teachers use computers is to run Computer Assisted Instruction (CAI) programs. This type of software has been designed to teach a student or to present information to a student. The first three sections of this chapter cover varieties of CAI. *Drill-and-practice* software asks questions, tells you if your responses are correct or not, and sometimes calculates the percentage of answers you got right. *Tutorials* give more feedback than drill and practice; they guide the student as they present a topic ("teaching" it, if you will). *Simulations* present situations based on real life and let students manipulate factors involved in them.

It is often impossible to distinguish absolutely between these three kinds of software. Any piece of software may include drill work, and programs may use simulation to enhance any presentation. Nevertheless, we feel that the concepts involved in these three modes of CAI are distinct enough to warrant a separate discussion of each.

CAI guides the student through some type of learning process with a preprogrammed activity, but the computer can also be controlled by students and teachers for their own purposes, and the second part of the chapter deals with some of these applications. Data bases, or large collections of information stored on disks, can be accessed for research. Computers can be connected to each other through telephone lines in order to communicate with other computer users or to obtain information. Better essay writing and research can be promoted by using the computer as a word processor.

All of these applications are intended for students to use under a teacher's supervision. Another category is computer software designed solely for the teacher. Teachers can use computers to keep student records or to design programs for students to run. The last section of the chapter presents some of these uses.

Software Selection and Organizing Computer Use

Throughout the chapter, in order to make the discussions more concrete, we refer to specific pieces of software that are on the market. By naming certain products we do not intend to imply that these are the best or the only ones to use: Literally thousands of educational programs have been published. We have tried, however, to choose software that we feel might most profitably be used by social studies teachers. Thus, although our choices were selective, they are not at all exhaustive.

We have included in this book another way for you to get to know about software. The "Guide to Resources" in the appendix provides information about software, software publishers, publications that review software, teacher groups and networks, and more.

In using computers in the classroom, knowing what kind of software is available is only part of the teacher's problem. It is also essential to know how to evaluate software and how to deal with the limitations of computer equipment. For example, Should everyone in the class use the software? What if there is only one computer for the whole class? Should students work alone or in groups? Should all of the computers be in a central location?

Whenever possible we have tried to deal with these kinds of questions in separate sections on computer applications, since criteria for evaluating drill-and-practice software and the ways you might use it are to some extent unique to drill and practice. There are also specific features to look for in word processing software that are not relevant, say, to networking programs.

The way you organize your computers may also depend on the use to which they are put. A central computer lab with all of the machines networked to each other so that they all run the same program may be very appropriate for drill or other kinds of CAI software but is not necessarily good for using data bases. If your school gives you one computer for your classroom, you may decide that a certain drill program (which doesn't take too long to do) can be used by all of the students one-by-one (or in small groups). Alternatively, you may decide to use the computer for demonstrations presented to the whole class, especially if you have large-screen output for it.

These are the kinds of questions that must be answered by teachers when using any media or any piece of equipment. The primary question must be, Is this software something I want to use? And, if it is, then a set of questions follows: Who should use it — everyone, or a selected group of students? Given the limitations in equipment, should students use it one-by-one, in small groups, or as a whole class? How much time should you devote to it? Since the content of software is closely related to its use, throughout this chapter we have tried to integrate these issues into the discussion.

☐ DRILL AND PRACTICE ☐

Educational Value

Drill and practice is a type of learning activity certainly by no means unique to the social studies. When practicing almost any new skill, we often engage in some form of drill to help us integrate the skill into our working knowledge. We use drill frequently in school in all subject areas and in various forms: flash cards; workbook exercises; rote learning through spoken, written, and sung repetition; and in many learning games.

Historically, the first efforts in educational software were of the drill-and-practice type. When computer storage was more limited and more expensive than today, it was economical to use the computer as a flash card or a question-and-answer screen. Drill work involves few decisions for the computer to make, so it is easy to program. A set of questions and the correct responses must be stored. For each question asked, the response must be matched against the correct answer. No further branching of the program is necessary.

At first, most educational software programs were for math and science, since computers have traditionally been associated with these subjects. Just as teachers used arithmetic flash cards, programs soon abounded that flashed addition and multiplication facts on the screen. In recent years, as the computer has come to be seen also as a social studies tool, the earliest software efforts in this area were also in drill work. Many early programs dealt with state capitals.

Fortunately this is no longer the whole story. As computer storage capability and processing power have increased, programs that require decision making, graphic representation, and use of large quantities of data have become possible. At the same time, however, drill-and-practice programs are relatively easy and inexpensive to produce, and a large proportion of new software is of this type.

Drill-and-practice Software

Drill-and-practice software does not all look alike. Although earlier software consisted solely of text on the screen, newer computer graphic capabilities have given recent software more varied features. In this section we are going to look at three examples of drill-and-practice software. Two of these, SMALLTOWN USA and CAPITALS OF STATES, draw maps on which to locate specific sites. The third, THE DECADES GAME, uses only text to present a game for one to four players. Although we won't go into minute detail about each of these programs, we will try to present their main features in order to bring out many of the varied possibilities that drill and practice holds for students using microcomputers.

THE DECADES GAME.   This software package, designed for use in high school, consists of three disks, each containing 6 games, making 18 games in all. Each of the games has the same format. Up to four people can play. You can choose the number of rounds (decades) in the game. In each round, you (or you and your opponents) are presented with events that occurred in a single decade of American history. As each event is presented on the screen, each player guesses the decade in which it occurred. Thus, if the event is "John Adams becomes president," you would type the date 1790, since the event occurred in that decade.

Each player gets a chance at each event. If all the players get the decade wrong, another event is presented — up to four events per round. If one or more players gets the answer right, that round is over, and the updated players' scores are shown. When the round ends, either through someone's getting the right answer or everyone's missing all four events, the correct decade is shown. A player receives points in each round according to how quickly he or she identifies the decade.

That is the essence of the game. Each of the 18 games contains different facts, and each time you play each game the events may be presented in a different order. When you answer incorrectly, you are not told the correct answer right away, but you are allowed to keep trying to identify the correct decade. With each successive guess, the job supposedly becomes easier, because you already know something about the decade.

A large range of types of events is used, from facts that every American history textbook covers ("Abraham Lincoln was the first president to be assassinated") to less familiar information ("Grant Wood paints *American Gothic*"). As such, it has seemed to some people that THE DECADES GAME is a trivia game. Others have enjoyed it as a valuable historical drill, mixing political, military, and cultural events together so that the student gets a sense of their happening in the same decade. (It is interesting to note that the authors did not choose to make a game of guessing the actual dates.)

The instructions for this game are all contained on the disk. When beginning the program, you are given the option of reading the directions or not. The directions take several screens to present, because of complexities in scoring and turn taking, but the game really boils down to identifying the approximate dates of many events in American history.

CAPITALS OF STATES.   This software package, designed for junior high school, is even simpler to describe than THE DECADES GAME. As its name implies, this program drills you on the names of capitals of the states in the United States. To begin with, you are given choices: Which region of the United States do you want to try, and how many questions do you want? Then an outline map of the states in the region that you selected is drawn on the screen (New England, Atlantic Coast, the West, and so forth), and a dot blinks on and off in one of the states, marking the state capital.

You respond to the blinking dot by typing the name of the capital of that state. You get only one attempt per state, and you must spell the name of the capital correctly. However, if you answer incorrectly, the question may be asked again before you finish playing. When you finish the number of states you requested, you are told the percentage you got correct and asked if you want another turn.

The reason that this program deals with only one section of the country at a time is that a computer screen is too small to adequately portray all of the states and still make the smallest ones distinct. In addition, the resolution of most microcomputer screens is not great, which means that some state boundary lines that are straight look jagged, and what are supposed to be curved lines are clearly composed of small straight lines. Scale, of course, is also affected by the size of the computer screen. The larger the drawing, the easier it is to compensate for the distortions. So, look-ing at only one region at a time allows for a more accurate picture of the map of the United States.

This use of graphics lends some interest to drill and practice. The computer's power to draw, erase, and redraw, combined with its ability to randomize (change the order in which it presents the states each time) provides variety. No text is needed with the map outline: The drawing and the blinking dot clue the player. The software is simple but does just what it sets out to do: provide drill and practice in naming the state capitals.

One question that is often asked about educational (or any) software is, Do I need a computer to do this? Ultimately you will have to answer this for yourself when considering any particular program. For now, con-sider what CAPITALS OF STATES does, and ask yourself if any other tool (paper, cards, blackboard, book) would do as well. One factor to keep in mind in this regard is that students often like the very act of working on the computer, at least in the beginning; seeing lines appear and disappear, typing responses, getting immediate feedback, and waiting for the next question, are fascinating. It is not yet known for sure whether this effect (often called the "halo" effect) will wear off with greater familiarity with the computer.

Another important consideration is price: Does what the software pur-ports to do justify paying so much for it? In this case, however, price is not a factor. There is a body of software in the public domain, developed to be used by anyone, of which CAPITALS OF STATES is an example.

SMALLTOWN USA.   In this program (designed for teaching elementary school map skills), graphics are used in a special way. A map of several blocks of a fictitious town called Smalltown is shown on the computer screen. On this map the streets are labeled, a set of buildings is drawn, and various buildings are identified with one or two initials. *RR* stands for railroad, *PO* for post office, and so forth.

A map key or legend also appears on the screen at first, and you get to review the key before you start answering questions. (Once the ques-tioning begins, the key is no longer shown.) An introduction also explains and demonstrates how to count the number of blocks one must travel, which is one of the main points of the program. To get from the post office to the railroad station, for instance, a little stick figure moves along the streets, leaving a trail of 1s on the first block, 2s on the second block, and so on, until it arrives at its destination. A portion of a block is counted as a block.

Once familiar with the map, the student is taken through questions about six of the buildings located on the map. For each building, three questions with the same format are asked. For example:

1. What street is the bakery on?
2. Bob [the child's name is inserted by the computer after an opening query] will leave the train station and walk to the bakery. How many blocks will Bob walk?
3. At the bakery Bob can:
   a. Buy bread
   b. Mail a letter
   c. Buy groceries

An important question to ask of any instructional software is, How are incorrect answers handled? (For this reason, when evaluating software, it's a good idea to spend a lot of time getting answers wrong.) In SMALLTOWN USA, much of the activity comes from incorrect answers. If the third, multiple choice question is answered incorrectly, the correct answer is simply presented. The first two questions, however, lend themselves to using the map for a more graphic error correction. In the first case, after two incorrect attempts to name the street where the bakery is, the program highlights and flashes the street and its name. If the student cannot count the number of blocks (again in two attempts), the program counts them out, as it did in the introduction, by animating a little figure that moves along the route and leaves numbers behind it.

In this piece of software, the introduction and presentation of the map are fairly elaborate: There is much detail for the student to absorb. The heart of the program, though, is this set of three questions, repeated for different map locations.

Classroom Use of Drill-and-practice Software

There are many important pedagogical and practical issues that teachers must think about when considering the use of this kind of software. Let's review some of them.

Do I Need Drill-and-practice Software? Another way of putting this question is to ask yourself, Can I do the same thing as well or better without a computer? Ultimately, each piece of software must be evaluated on its own merits. You might decide that in some cases flash cards would do just as well. The more general question of whether computers should be used for drill and practice has been debated by experts. Some argue that computers have the potential of doing much more than drill and that the other types of instructional activities discussed in this chapter are more valuable. On the other hand, some feel that drill work is exactly the type of activity that the computer does best. How much time one spends on drill in class varies from teacher to teacher, but it seems clear that we all do some of it. Let's look at some of the criteria you might use for evaluating individual pieces of software.

Is the Activity Clear?   Included in this broad question are these considerations: Are the goals of the drill clearly set out? Does the software try to do too much? Are the directions easy to follow? Software is sometimes criticized for being too simple: It is easy, and tempting, for programmers to throw in more and more activity. Often, however, the simpler the better: A program that drills math facts or state capitals and tries to do nothing more may be just what you think you need.

Is the Format a Help or a Hindrance?   Format refers to the way the software is presented on the screen: screen layout, use of color and sound, graphics, speed of presentation, and so on. One must evaluate whether the effects that a program uses detract from the activity. SMALLTOWN USA and CAPITALS OF STATES need the graphics they use for their activities. Many other drill programs add on graphics for effects that are unnecessary for the drill. A current fad is to put the drill facts on spaceships and have students "shoot them down" by answering questions. Is this format designed to enhance the learning or remembering of facts?

Who Should Use the Software?   Drill and practice may be used at any age to consolidate learning, and such software is designed for all ages. Among the programs presented in this section, SMALLTOWN USA, as we have seen, is designed primarily for elementary school, CAPITALS OF STATES for junior high school, and THE DECADES GAME for high school. However, as with any material, teachers will use them wherever appropriate, and the creators of most software packages are quick to point out that their programs may be useful with students of various ages.

How Do I Use Drill-and-practice Software in a Class?   Schools adopt many strategies for sharing software among students. Some set up learning labs with many computers, so that many students can work on the same program at once. Within this possibility, a school might connect (or network) all the computers together, so that one master machine controls what everyone does. This way only one disk is needed. Or several different programs may be used with different computers. It is not always necessary for all the students to be doing the same work at the same time.

In the classroom, one sometimes finds one or a few computers. In this case, a possibility would be to have students take turns using any individual piece of software, either singly or in small groups. Teachers can, and probably should, demonstrate the software to groups or the whole class before leaving it to the students. Schools often opt to rotate machines from class to class in weekly or monthly shifts.

What About Cost? After you have decided that a certain program would be useful, you must still consider its cost. Does the price make it less feasible than using more traditional materials for the same purpose, even though you may like certain features of the software? Low cost is usually one factor in favor of drill-and-practice software. Compared to other software, at least, drill programs are generally less expensive, because they are shorter, require less memory space for data, graphics, and so forth, and therefore are easier to design and produce. Enhancing the drill by adding graphics can also add to expense, but you can expect the cost of these disks to range generally from very little ($10 to $20) up to possibly $50 to $70.

Putting all the factors together is never easy, and there are certainly many more things to consider than are discussed here. What is probably the single most important consideration is whether a teacher believes that any single activity is worthwhile. This decision must be made on the basis of carefully considering the activity itself and should not be influenced by outside pressure to use computers or to buy a certain amount of software. Ideally, teachers should be able to view the software before they are expected to send their students off to use it.

☐   TUTORIALS   ☐

Using the computer to tutor a student in a skill or a content area is still something of a new frontier for social studies. Virtually no commercial programs of this type are widely available for social studies at this writing, although some programs do have tutorial elements. (James Lengel has written some software to accompany his book *Law and American History*, which tutors students about the legal roots of our civil rights (see the "Guide to Resources" in the appendix). Much of the drill-and-practice software that is now available has no tutorial introduction. For example, in CAPITALS OF STATES students are not shown a map of the United States with the state names indicated before they are asked to name the state capitals, nor can they refer back to a map to help themselves remember where the states are in relation to each other. Such a tutorial introduction would, of course, require additional programming and computer memory.

Tutorial programs also require something that most social studies teachers don't yet have: access to many computers. Most tutorials in other subject areas are written with the idea that there will be one student using each program on one computer. Tutorials used for remediation certainly would not require every student in the class to have one-to-one access to a computer, but introducing a new skill or concept probably would mean the use of many computers, unless the program was written to be used by groups or teams of students.

Once the question of access is worked out, though, almost any basic social studies skill could become the subject of a piece of tutorial software. For example, a program written to tutor elementary students in cardinal directions might contain an explanation of what the concepts of north, south, east, and west are and how they apply to the earth and maps. The skill of finding directions on a map might be practiced by checking student input against a predetermined route on a town map. The skill might be applied by using a game in which two fire trucks are "driven" by students through town, using NORTH, SOUTH, EAST, and WEST commands to guide the trucks to the fires that need to be put out.

The basic advantage of using the computer to tutor students is the instant feedback that they can receive as they work their way through the complexities and practical applications of using a new skill. Workbooks and other similar printed materials require more teacher introduction and follow-up. Unfortunately, often by the time the teacher has had a chance to correct the workbook exercises, students may have already become confused about a skill. Tutorial software can also allow students to work at their own pace. In the case of many of the social studies skills, the remedial value of tutorial software is that students could quickly review many of the skills they do not use all the time, such as map skills. Students could also receive a chance to get more guided practice in a certain skill.

The graphic capabilities of the computer also add a new dimension to learning social studies skills. For example, with computer animation a student could determine the actual scale on a map, in order to make distance measurements. Overlays for maps could help students to test out hypotheses about the relationship between climate and products. Split-screen capabilities could help students to compare maps, charts, and other graphic information more easily. If it is possible to call up various kinds of maps and charts to the screen, students can easily begin to make very graphic, visual comparisons between countries or regions, adding a global dimension to any content area.

Examples such as those just mentioned are only now beginning to be developed for the market. The problem at this point is that unless more computers become available to social studies students, tutorial software will probably be rather slow to develop. Some of the applications suggested here would also be rather expensive to implement because of the research and programming time and difficulty involved. Publishers do seem to be interested in electronic "workbooks," but at this point the translation from print to computer has not taken advantage of some of the special capabilities that the computer has to offer.

One bright spot is that with a little programming expertise — and, of course, the investment of some time — classroom teachers can quite easily put together a variety of tutorial software. Authoring languages (simplified programming languages for constructing instructional software) are also a simple way to devise this type of software. In this area, one of the most important considerations is, of course, that the special capabilities of the computer are being used, and that what is being presented is not just print materials typed into the computer for students to use to merely fill in the blanks.

☐   SIMULATIONS   ☐

Educational Value

Certainly, an ideal way to teach history would be to load students into a time machine and take them back into the past to witness or take part in important events, to meet outstanding leaders, and to experience other cultures. Unfortunately, current technology is not quite up to such ventures, but computer simulations are one tool that social studies teachers can use to help students empathize with other people from different times and places and to give them an opportunity to try to analyze and solve current, past, and future problems.

To simulate is to imitate, and to imitate is one of the things that the computer does best. This is perhaps why some of the best software developed so far for the social studies is in the area of simulations. Everything from a trip out West in the 1840s to the making of a president in the 1980s has been devised, and bigger and better simulations are promised for the future.

A simple definition of a simulation is that it is a model that can be manipulated. All of us have had experiences with simulations, starting with playing house as young children. The family model, along with the roles of each of its individual members, is one of the first systems that children imitate and analyze in detail. To make the model work, they bring their own experiences of family life to bear, along with what they have observed of other families in person, in books, and on television. The decision making that goes on during the game—who goes off to work, who stays home with the children, and how the roles of family members are played out—all is based on observation, logic, and personal experience.

Adults have come up with some more sophisticated simulations. Social scientists have been using simulations to analyze the cause and effects of social problems for years. In the late 1960s and early 1970s, computer models were proposed as ways of analyzing and solving important social and economic problems. *The Limits to Growth*, by Dennis Meadows, and others, examined the WORLD 3 model and the possible relationships between population, pollution, resource depletion, and economic growth. *Urban Dynamics*, by Jay Forrester, used a computer model to probe the causes of urban growth and decay and the effects of urban renewal programs. Both models broke down the problems into a variety of factors and manipulated these factors to predict what the effects would be. Some criticism came for oversimplifying problems that involve numerous individual human factors.

Most social studies teachers who have used written simulations know that this simplification of factors is one of the advantages of using a simulation. A simulation can make a complicated problem seem simple by highlighting certain facts, concepts, skills, and interactions, so that the student is not overwhelmed with petty details. Simulations can also speed up long-drawn-out events (such as the negotiation of a treaty, or the conduct of an election) or slow down swiftly occurring but complicated events (such as an involved conflict with many factors, or an intricate business transaction), in order to let students more clearly observe the process and the results. Simulations are also certainly safer, cheaper, and much easier to transport into the classroom than the actual process, too.

The computer is an ideal tool to use to simulate situations. In using many written simulations, a referee of sorts is often required. The teacher usually takes on this role, while at the same time trying to encourage other activities and keep order. In most computer simulations, the computer takes on this job and has little trouble playing the unbiased, passive lawgiver and lawmaker. The computer is also fast and doesn't have to shuffle through cards or papers to find the right materials. Often, more factors can be addressed in a computer simulation because the computer has little problem remembering all the details or doing calculations. Students can also see the results of their decisions very quickly. Another advantage of using the computer is that, properly programmed, it can keep track of where you were in a simulation when class ended and can begin again exactly at that spot when class resumes the next day, the next week, or the next month.

Some teachers are uncomfortable with simulations because they seem to be games or because they don't fit into the traditional lecture/reading/report method of teaching social studies. Frankly, students also tend to make some noise when involved in simulation because they are interacting with each other and can become quite exuberant at times as their fortunes rise or fall in the course of the simulation.

The experience of taking part in a simulation, though, can change passive learning into active understanding of the concepts and skills being taught. Simulations, whether of the computer-enhanced or paper-and-pencil variety, are not intended as a replacement for more traditional methods of teaching social studies. They are intended instead to supplement them and to give students a chance to apply their knowledge and skills to certain kinds of problem-solving situations. For example, after a traditional introduction to map skills, a computer simulation might be used to have students apply their skills by going on a rescue mission or exploring uncharted territory.

Very few simulations (let alone computer simulations) can stand on their own as complete lessons or units. All of them have to be introduced and supplemented by readings, discussions, lectures, and other activities. If you keep your objectives for the simulation in mind, this can be done quite easily, and the simulation can be used like any other single lesson that is part of a unit or sequence.

Simulation Software

As a guide to using and evaluating computer simulations, in this section we look at three of the better-known and most readily available ones: OREGON TRAIL, GEOGRAPHY SEARCH, and PRESIDENT ELECT. Each of these simulations comes with paper documentation on how to use the software in the classroom.

OREGON TRAIL. This simulation program was developed by the Minnesota Educational Computing Consortium and is on a disk of social studies simulations for elementary school students. The simulation opens in 1847 in Independence, Missouri, where students are asked to spend $900 on supplies to be used for a journey over the Oregon Trail to Oregon City. A budget sheet for oxen, food, ammunition, clothing, and miscellaneous supplies appears on the screen for students — who can work either individually or as a group — to use in planning what they are going to spend their limited funds for. Some advice is given on choices: for example, students are told that spending more money for better oxen that can move faster would be a good investment. Students are also cautioned that they can either spend all of their money before they start their trip or save some of their cash to spend along the way at forts if their supplies run low. Supplies at forts (the forerunners of convenience stores) are, of course, more expensive, and hunting is another option students have along the way to obtain more food.

Each turn begins with a message giving the day's date (in 1847); a status report on stocks of food, bullets, clothing, various other supplies, and cash; and mileage figures. Students are asked whether they want to hunt, to stop at the next fort, or to continue. If they choose to hunt, they take shots at running deer. If hit, the deer adds to their food supply. Each shot depletes the bullet supply. If they want to stop at a fort, they are given the chance to buy supplies. All of these stops, of course, slow them down as they try to make it through the mountains before the snows come.

If they choose to continue along the trail, the students are asked whether they want to eat poorly, moderately well, or very well. Their choice usually has no immediate effect, but if they choose to eat poorly too many times they increase their chance of getting sick on the journey. At the end of most turns, the students receive a message about what happened that day on the trail. These random messages can be anything from a stuck wagon and lost supplies to a poisonous snakebite or a blizzard. All of these messages are reflected in a reduction of the supplies and in delays and loss of time on the trail.

The wagon train can also be attacked by hostile riders or wild animals. Students are given a choice of tactics to use, including running, counterattacking, continuing, or circling the wagons. The consequences of these tactics are flashed on the screen immediately after the students make their decisions.

If students are lucky enough to make the 2,040-mile journey successfully, the computer lets them know that they have done so with a congratulatory message from President Polk. If they don't make it and die along the way, the computer queries whether they would like to have a minister and a fancy funeral or to have their next of kin informed, charges them accordingly, and wishes them better luck next time.

OREGON TRAIL was one of the first simulations developed for the social studies. It was constructed by a social studies teacher named Don Rawitsch, who used primary and secondary source materials to make the simulation as authentic as possible. Many of the elements of misfortune that occurred on the trail were culled from diaries and additional primary sources that are cited in the user manual available from the Minnesota Educational Computing Consortium.

Certainly OREGON TRAIL could not stand alone as the only material presented on the trials and tribulations of the trek to the West in the 1840s, but, properly supplemented by other readings, it can give younger students a chance to comprehend how dangerous such a journey was. It can also lead to an interesting discussion of models of reality. How do we form our images of what life was like in the past? How is this computer version of life on the trail different from or similar to the images students have formed previously from watching television, seeing movies, or reading a textbook? What would students include if they had to make up simulations of their own family life for students of the future to use?

Because teams can use this simulation, it is easy to use with larger groups of students, getting around the problem of limited access to multiple computers. Interesting social interaction can take place while the game is in progress as teams grapple with the issues of how decisions should be made and how the work will be done. These interactive skills add to the simulation experience.

GEOGRAPHY SEARCH. In this simulation, junior and senior high school students become the crews of sailing ships who have been sent out to the New World to look for gold by their queen. The precise time setting for the simulation is never really made clear, but from the tools available for navigating the ship we realize that it takes place before or about the time of Columbus. The navigation of the ship is managed by observing natural phenomena including the position of the North Star (to determine latitude); the length and position of shadows (to determine longitude); the depth of the water (to determine proximity to land); and weather (to determine where the trade winds are). The goal of each crew is to sail to the New Territory, to retrieve the gold (and avoid pirates), and to be the first back to be rewarded handsomely by the queen.

The simulation begins with each crew meeting privately to determine where they are, which way they will go (determined by wind direction), and how long they are going to sail. Each crew enters these decisions into the computer, which then issues a status report on the ship, showing wind direction and speed; position of the North Star in the night sky above the horizon, shown as a blinking dot on the screen; the length of the shadow of the ship during the day; the depth of the water; the amount of supplies left; and the weather, including the temperature. If the ship is near land, the status report also includes information on vegetation.

All of this information remains on the screen for only 30 seconds, so each member of the crew must concentrate on grasping the information for which he or she is responsible. This quick display of information is a very effective device for making the crew members dependent upon each other, since no one person alone can take in all the information needed for making the decisions about where the ship is and how it should proceed. During the first few turns, though, this rapid display can be very disconcerting to students who have never had to depend on each other for successful completion of a classroom exercise.

After their turn at the computer, crew members meet again privately to fill in the data sheets and to plot their location on the maps provided with the simulation. They again make decisions, based on the data, to determine what they will do when it is their turn at the computer. The computer also diagrams the location of each ship at the end of a crew's turn. This lets crews have a chance to note where they are in relation to their opponents or to pirates who might be lurking ready to snatch their gold or supplies.

When a ship finally reaches land, the crew is given the option of going ashore for supplies or of going into the City of Gold (once they have located it) to pick up the treasure they have come for. With supplies and gold on board, crews usually turn to head home, sailing in the opposite direction to the one they came from or continuing on to discover for themselves whether the world really is round.

It usually takes 10 to 12 rounds, over several days, to complete a voyage, but students are learning much more than geography when they are using GEOGRAPHY SEARCH. Using this simulation to accompany what is often a rote presentation of explorers, dates, and areas explored can give students an opportunity to experience the uncertainty faced by the early explorers and to appreciate the hardships and obstacles they faced.

Many of the geographic terms, as well as concepts such as longitude, latitude, weather, and navigation, take on new meaning when students are making practical use of them. Being forced into group decision making is also a helpful experience for many students who have never had to depend on others in the classroom for success before. It is also interesting to watch how some of the mecker members of a class take on a new importance because their piece of data might hold the key to the group's failure or success.

GEOGRAPHY SEARCH is also a well-planned simulation, because the software is designed to let you turn the computer off at the end of a class session and turn it on to where you left off, when class resumes. Because it is set up to be played by teams, one computer can serve the entire class (there is the option of using six ships with crews of four to six members). The flexibility of GEOGRAPHY SEARCH is an important model for the designers of social studies software. If only a few computers are available to a social studies teacher, the team approach makes classroom management much easier when the entire class can be involved in using one computer at the same time.

PRESIDENT ELECT.   This is a simulation of a presidential campaign during the nine-week period from Labor Day to Election Day in November. The goal of the simulation is to get your candidate (or yourself) elected by using a variety of strategies. The simulation contains a data base of information on certain leading political figures who might be chosen to run (giving their strengths, weaknesses, track records, and so forth) and on how elections have been effected by particular campaign strategies in the past.

When the disk is inserted, the program gives the option of starting a new game, continuing a saved game, demonstrating the graphics, or watching a demonstration of the 1960 campaign, without player participation. As discussed before, being able to start and stop a simulation is a bonus. Being able to view a demonstration is a good option for reviewing the game before you play it with students.

When starting a new game, the program constructs a scenario on the state of the Union. By requesting data on the economy and world conditions, you choose two or three candidates to run against each other under those circumstances. Candidates can be chosen irrespective of their party or actual time frame, meaning that even George McGovern could run as a Republican. If information about the candidate (who could be a class member) is not contained in the program's data base, the candidate is "interviewed" by the computer to obtain his or her positions on particular issues and to find the candidate's position on the political spectrum. It is possible to play against the computer by letting it manage the other candidate(s) or run the whole election by itself.

The election campaign is nine weeks (turns) long, and to go through a complete campaign takes about 1½ to 2 hours. Each week the campaign staffs, made up of teams of students, receive poll results that show the national popular vote and state-by-state standings. During the campaign, the campaign staffs and their candidates try to improve on their positions through the expenditure of campaign funds on overhead, advertising, campaign stops, and foreign travel. The candidates are also given an opportunity to debate. Media ratings on who was strong or weak then become part of the input on the race.

Campaign funds are limited, and as each turn progresses each candidate and staff must decide how to spend their funds. Overhead is unavoidable. Advertising is divided into national, regional, and individual state campaigns, with each having a different cost and a potentially unique effect on the race. Campaign stops cost varying amounts, and each candidate must beware of fatigue. Foreign visits are a gamble; sometimes they backfire on the candidate. At the end of each week, strengths are adjusted on the basis of the decisions that the candidates and their staffs have made and the other events of the week. Each new week begins with a new set of standings. After the ninth week, the results of the election are tabulated by the computer, and a winner is declared. This can be simulated in realtime (4 to 6 hours), or the votes can be tallied in less than 15 seconds.

One of the unique features of PRESIDENT ELECT is the inclusion of a data base of background on candidates and historical information on elections. Although the computer is the neutral moderator of the election process, it also, by using this information, keeps the election process very realistic. Thoughtful decisions have to be made on the part of campaign staffs to sway the results to favor one candidate over the other. The computer becomes the "great electorate"—way out there somewhere.

PRESIDENT ELECT does make an excellent culminating activity when a class is studying the Constitution and the electoral process—especially the electoral college. The capabilities of the computer are used very well as the computer becomes the moderator, calculator, and historian and can quickly and graphically display the changing election scene—from poll results to maps of which states belong to which candidates or are neutral. Introduced and supplemented properly, PRESIDENT ELECT can also lend an air of reality that is so often missing to off–election-year presentations of presidential politics.

The only unrealistic thing about PRESIDENT ELECT is the amount of campaign funds that are spent—only hundreds of dollars rather than thousands. This makes the management of funds easier and dollar amount input simpler, but it should be pointed out to students how expensive running a presidential campaign really is today. A discussion of the kind of financial resources or backing a candidate must have to be considered a candidate with clout should also be part of the debriefing.

Evaluating Simulations

It is difficult, if not impossible, to formally evaluate the results of the learning going on during the use of computer simulations such as those described here. The final outcomes arrived at by the groups or individuals that use them can only begin to indicate how well students are learning from their exposure to the cause-and-effect relationships with which they are working. The social interaction that goes on during all three of the simulations reviewed here is essential to the success of the simulations, but, beyond the conclusions reached by carefully observing the groups, it is impossible to formally document. Examination of the worksheets that students are using during the process will give you some idea of how things are going but again will not give you a truly objective picture of the results.

It is likely that using computer simulations will have other kinds of payoffs. The class that has been exposed to having to cooperate with each other to successfully complete a task may transfer those skills to other experiences both inside and outside the classroom. Practical applications of budgeting skills or geography concepts may have some carryover effect in ways that can be more formally tested and evaluated.

As has already been mentioned, simulations can also make history become more real. After using each of these simulations, some students have been motivated to try to find out more about each topic. For example, after using GEOGRAPHY SEARCH, students have become more interested in learning what life was like for the explorers, the cultures of the foreign peoples they encountered, how navigation has improved, and how modern "explorers" in the space shuttle use some of the same navigational methods employed by students using the simulation. This heightened interest is very gratifying to any teacher.

The Future of Simulations

Computer simulations are only just beginning to emerge as tools for the social studies teacher. As was mentioned earlier, not every teacher is comfortable using a simulation, because of the game connotation and because the results cannot always be formally evaluated. Simulations also encourage student interaction, which can create a noisy and hectic (but controllable) classroom atmosphere.

In discussing each of the three simulations included here, we have mentioned some things to look out for when evaluating a simulation program. Two key considerations are to determine how easy the program is to use and how well documented it is. The directions for use of the simulation should also be clear and straightforward, so that you know what to expect even before you turn on the machine.

Unlike drill-and practice and tutorial software, computer simulations are rather difficult for teachers to design and program on their own. A book that can help, though, is *An Introduction to Computer Simulations*, by Nancy Roberts, (see the "Guide to Resources" in the appendix, for more information). Written for junior or senior high school students, this book can serve as an introduction to what goes on in a computer simulation and as a guide to writing computer simulations.

Having students build their own simulation models must be seen as the ultimate goal of using simulations in social studies education. Armed with a variety of dates, students can ask their own "what if" questions and analyze problems of both past, present, and future societies. This may not be so far down the road, as our students begin to hone their programming skills.

☐   **ON-SITE DATA BASES**   ☐

Educational Value

The word *data* (the plural of *datum*) has come down to us from the ancient Romans and refers to facts that we use to draw conclusions. Because modern science has popularized the term, we have come to associate data primarily with numbers and measurements. For a scientific conclusion to be regarded as valid today, large samples of data must be collected, correlated, and used as proof. All of us, though, use data from the world around us all of the time.

Computers are the perfect tools for storing and manipulating data. The computer's storage capability is large and constantly growing: Hundreds of thousands of bytes (equivalent to letters) of information can easily be stored on current microcomputer disks. With the latest technology, already fast processing speeds, which now range in the millions of operations per second, are being even further improved.

Technically, all information that a computer uses is its data, no matter whether the information comes from the user's input or is already stored inside the computer program. In this section, however, we are concerned with large amounts of data that are stored in an organized way so that they can be easily accessed. Data stored in this way are called *data bases*.

An example of a common computer program that uses a data base is the recipe-storing program, which recently helped to sell many microcomputers to busy cooks. This kind of program allows you to enter such data as the ingredients you have on hand or information about a recipe you are searching for, such as what type of food it is for. When the data have been entered, the program can access the data base to look up an individual recipe or to list all the recipes that contain those particular ingredients. It can also list all the desserts in its memory or plan sample meals, and so on. The program organizes the data you type in so that the computer can sort through it easily, categorize it, and match it up with what you are looking for.

Increasingly, institutions in our society use large data bases. The U.S.

Census Bureau, the Internal Revenue Service, insurance companies, and credit companies are only a few of the organizations that could not function in the modern world without huge amounts of data stored on large computers. Imagine how difficult it would be for government planners to predict population trends without computers: For example, how long would it take to average the ages of all citizens who live in large urban areas without computers?

As the amount of information used by computers has multiplied in our society, we have become aware of many problems that they raise. How are data about people being used, and by whom? How can individual privacy be protected? These issues (discussed in Chapter 4) apply whether one is using data on a microcomputer or on the government's largest mainframe computer.

For our purposes, it is convenient to discuss the classroom applications of on-site and off-site data bases separately. In this section we discuss the use of on-site data bases, in which all of the data is stored right where you are, on disks that your microcomputer can access. The following section of the chapter deals with those applications in which larger data bases are needed; these are located off-site in some central computer, and you access them by connecting your microcomputer with the central source via telephone lines.

There is a great deal of interest in using data bases in the social studies, and much of the current work in software development is being done in this area. In this section we will consider three kinds of data-base programs that could be useful. In the first one, called SUPERMAP, the data base is already stored in the disk and cannot be altered or added to. The purpose of the SUPERMAP program is to present this stored information in different ways on maps of the United States. In both of the other programs we will look at, you enter all the data yourself, but with different purposes in mind. In POLLS AND POLITICS, the data you enter are used to conduct polls, and the program graphs the results. The other program, Apple Computer Company's PERSONAL FILING SYSTEM, is a general-purpose filing program that lets you define the records you keep and then processes and presents the data to you in a variety of ways. We have selected these three programs because of the variety of ways in which they make use of data bases and because they are all simple to use.

Applied Data Bases

SUPERMAP. The data contained in the SUPERMAP program consists of information about over 300 cities in the United States. For each of these cities, a variety of information is stored: the city's name, the state it is in, population figures for 1970, zip code numbers, area code, time zone, and latitude and longitude. The program lets the user locate any city on a map of the United States and displays all this information about the city beneath the map. The user types in the name of a city, and if it is in the data base, a dot will blink on the right spot on the map.

If this were all the program did, its usefulness would be limited to familiarizing students with the locations of cities. What makes SUPERMAP interesting is its presentation of the data in the form of graphic displays. SUPERMAP contains four different maps of the United States: an outline map of the states; a features map, outlining ecological patterns; and maps showing the mean solar radiation per day at ground level in January and July. A color monitor is almost a necessity for distinguishing one map area from another.

Using the map of the states, a student could find the answer to questions such as "What state is Akron in?" By switching maps, the student could also answer such questions as "Is Akron located in cropland, forest, grassland, desert, or swamp? How warm is Akron (on the average) in January and July?" Each of the maps, except the map of the states, shows a legend explaining what the different shading represents, so that one of the educational benefits of the program is learning to interpret a variety of map presentations.

With each of the maps, the user has a choice of activities. First, one can locate cities. (Each of these functions can be done regardless of what map one is looking at.) Second, the program can calculate the distance between any two cities. SUPERMAP shows this distance in miles and kilometers, and it also draws a line between the two cities. It does this slowly, with ascending or descending musical notes to represent a northward or southward journey. Third, the student can take a state capital quiz, naming the capitals of all of the states on the map (Alaska and Hawaii are not included). Fourth, the user can scan through the list of all of the more than three hundred cities, moving backward or forward; the program will blink for each city.

SUPERMAP, as we mentioned, contains a preexisting data base. This data base was put on the disk by the program's designers, and it cannot be modified. Since the programmers knew exactly what the data were and how they were organized, they were able to select the functions described above and present them as options. There are obviously many other things you might decide to do with such a data base. You might want to have more maps, for example, or you might want all the state capitals to be shown at the same time. SUPERMAP, of course, does only what its designers intended it to do, but it does it nicely and efficiently, with colorful graphics.

SUPERMAP could be used in a classroom in different ways. A teacher could use it to demonstrate to the whole class features of United States geography. A single child or even a small group could use it to find the answers to teacher-prepared questions. Or a student could access it to do research of his or her own.

SUPERMAP is a research tool. The state capital quiz is a bit of drill and practice, but all other options require the user to decide what to see. Like other research tools, it is probably best used by one or two students at a time. Thus it is the kind of software that requires only one computer; students can easily take turns using it.

As a research tool, it has advantages and disadvantages as compared to an encyclopedia, for instance. The encyclopedia contains a great deal more information than SUPERMAP — more quantity and variety of information, as well as more explanation of it. SUPERMAP, on the other hand, accesses its limited amount of data quickly and presents it graphically. It allows the user to select which data he or she wants to be presented at any time. It allows the user to erase maps at will and start over. Although limited in function, it presents information in a fairly dynamic way. A commercial software house, Focus Media, has also recently developed a map program called DEMOCOMP SERIES that allows students to do many of these functions with a wide variety of maps covering Europe, Asia, and Africa, as well as the United States (see the "Guide to Resources" in the appendix).

POLLS AND POLITICS.   There are a number of differences between SUPERMAP and POLLS AND POLITICS. SUPERMAP has a predefined data base and is used to answer questions about the data in it. It has only a few functions, which are easy to use; the few pages of documentation for the program are quite adequate. POLLS AND POLITICS, created by the Minnesota Educational Computing Consortium (MECC) for sixth through ninth graders, is meant to be an entire unit of classroom activity focusing on the subject of political polls. The documentation describes four classroom lessons containing activities concerning the history, uses, and evaluation of polls and how computers assist in taking polls and evaluating them. Also included are masters for transparencies, handouts, and quizzes. MECC has been active in developing classroom software for years, and from the start their philosophy has been to design programs that are integrated into regular classroom activity.

The data base in POLLS AND POLITICS, unlike that in SUPERMAP, is empty when you begin. The software has three parts. The first allows the user to define the questions for the poll and the acceptable responses. The second lets the user enter the data from the poll. The third part analyzes the data in two ways: by frequency distribution, in bar chart

form, or by tabulating the number of responses for each question compared to the number for every other (or cross-tabulating). Don't worry
if you don't know how these kinds of analyses work: The documentation
contains ample teacher preparation material, and the class lessons are designed to explain all parts of the process to students.

As we mentioned earlier, this software, like SUPERMAP, is simple for
the user to operate. This is because both of them are limited in number
of functions. There is usually a trade-off in software: The more it does
for you, the more you have to learn to use it, and the more chance there
is for error and confusion. POLLS AND POLITICS offers few options. For
instance, the DEFINE part of the program lets you define only 12 questions, with five responses each. You can enter the questions, change
them, delete them, or list them—and that's all. The ENTER and COUNT
sections are comparably simple. You can, by the way, print out any of
the results if you have a printer.

The simplicity of the software is compatible with its purpose. As an
introduction for students to the subject of political polls, the unit provides a lot of activity and stimulates a lot of thinking. The package is
designed to be an introduction to computers as well: It has computer
literacy learning objectives as well as social studies objectives. Students
learn about computer operation both from the lessons about how computers are used in poll taking and from using the software.

Filing Systems

Now we come to the most general kind of data base system—the kind
in which users make up the categories and enter the data, for whatever
purpose they choose. There are many versions of such filing systems on
the market, ranging from simple to complex in operation. Again, the principle applies that the simpler the system is, the less it will do for you.
Generally speaking, most filing systems will perform several functions.

First of all, however, you must define the organization of the file (or
data base). Suppose you want to keep a file of addresses and phone
numbers of friends. The information for each person will be called a
record, and within each record there will be several *fields* corresponding
to the types of information about each person. Typical fields for this file
might be name, address, and phone number. In addition, you might want
to break up the address field into street address; city; state; and zip code:
You will see why shortly.

After the file is defined, another section of the program lets you enter
the data for as many records as you want. These two functions are the
same as the DEFINE and ENTER functions of the POLLS AND POLITICS pro-

gram, except that now you can have a very large number of records, and many fields per record.

After your data is entered, you can start having fun with the file. Here are a few of the jobs your computer filing system can do for you:

Search through the records by field. That is, suppose you want to see the record of anyone named Bill, or anyone who lives on Main Street. Typing even a part of the field enables the computer to search through the records and find any that contain this information.

Sort by fields. You enter the data in any order you choose. The software can rearrange it for you in order of, say, zip code or any field that you name. This is why you might make zip code a separate field: If it were part of a larger, address field, you could not sort it separately.

Report. You specify which of the data from the file you want to see, and the computer will print out reports for you. For instance, you might want a report of only names and phone numbers, in alphabetical order.

Of the various filing systems on the market, one that is recommended for students is the Apple Computer Company's PERSONAL FILING SYSTEM (PFS). It is designed in modules, separate packages such as PFS:FILE; PFS:WRITE; PFS:REPORT, and others, which you must purchase separately. (They currently cost around $100 apiece.) The FILE software contains most of the functions of a good filing system, including the capacity to print out reports of records in the file. The advantage of the modular approach is that each module is manageable: You are not constantly faced with a multitude of options.

This is the main strength of PFS. There are only a few keystroke commands to learn. Beginners have been known to familiarize themselves with FILE sufficiently, in 15 minutes to half an hour, to use it effectively. There are some subtleties that take more study, but these are not necessary to begin with.

For these reasons, PFS might be a good beginning filer for students, possibly from late elementary school through high school. What could it be used for? The possibilities are practically limitless, for both students and teachers. While researching any topic, students might be encouraged to keep a data file on the information they collect. Learning how to store a large mass of data and then select out of it information relevant in a certain context is a valuable social studies skill. In addition, this process is invaluable in doing the research itself. One example might be creating a file of the different states in our country: their areas, populations, products, and so on. It would then be easy to select all of our states with populations over 5 million, or all those producing wheat. The research problems managed in this way can grow in complexity as students learn to handle the factors involved. A research file of this type already filled with facts about American history, U.S. HISTORY DATA FILES, has been developed by Beverly Hunter for the Scholastic Software Company and could be used as a model for student designing of data bases (see the "Guide to Resources" in the appendix).

Filing programs are proving invaluable for teachers as well. They can store records involving many aspects of students' school lives: addresses and scores, as well as attendance records. It might be useful to have your software tell you which students have missed more than 20 days of school, for instance.

Using On-site Data Bases

One feature that all these applications have in common is that data bases are usually used as research tools. Someone has created and stored a large amount of data in files, and the job of the software is to do something with that data: organize it, calculate with it, select from it, or present it in some way. The problem of the software designers is to make these functions useful to you. The three applications discussed here do this in different ways, but they all try to assist you in extracting information from large data bases.

What ages are these programs appropriate for? Only POLLS AND POLITICS offers a suggestion (grades 6 through 9), but in all cases, if students can understand the categories involved in keeping records, filing on the computer might be a useful activity.

In terms of classroom logistics, any use of on-line (computerized) data bases can be most easily accomplished by individuals or very small groups; these are not the types of activities that everyone must do at once. Thus they can be done even if there is only one computer in a classroom. With a suitable large-screen output, of course, they could also be used by teachers as demonstrations to teach the whole class the concepts involved.

At present, on-site data-base applications are limited. Effective use of a data base requires much data, and even though microcomputer disks hold hundreds of thousands of bytes of information, for many good applications this is not sufficient. To store much data you might need several disks, which means changing disks frequently in the middle of working. Disk technology, however, is constantly improving, so that newer disks contain many times more data than those of a few years ago. As this trend continues, we may expect the number of data-base applications to multiply as they become easier and cheaper to produce.

☐   OFF-SITE DATA BASES   ☐

Educational Value

So far, this book has examined software that is located in the school and resides "inside" the computer. In this section we will look at programs that exist outside of the computer and far away from the school.

Access to collections of information and data concerning society has always been essential for social studies. We seek to produce informed citizens who have the knowledge that they need to make wise decisions. We are responsible for transmitting important information about our culture and our form of government, and for keeping our students abreast of the world situation. In doing all of these things, we need to have access to, and store, enormous amounts of data and information.

Traditionally, the textbook and the library have served as the chief sources of information for the social studies, and both of these were located in the school. But these on-site, printed sources no longer hold a monopoly on the information that we need to teach our subject. Off-site collections of information, organized and indexed for rapid access, are today available "over the wire." They expand, rather than replace, the library and the textbook by providing more information, with better indexing, and up-to-the-minute currency.

On-line data bases have been with us for several decades. But until just recently, they were available only to well-funded libraries and to businesses with large computer operations. Today, a social studies teacher who has a microcomputer, a telephone line, and a few dollars can subscribe to a variety of resource files in several locations around the country. Although there are no off-site data bases designed solely for the social studies, there are many that contain information critical to social studies teaching. For example:

The Dow Jones News Service provides all the data and information that any economics student would ever need in order to keep informed about current business and industry.

News from around the world can be wired daily into your current events classroom through the New York Times Information Service and several other vendors.

History and biography files can be searched and printed out for the junior researcher through the DIALOG collection of data bases.

A periodical index more complete than the *Reader's Guide to Periodical Literature*, and electronically indexed in addition, can help students and teachers locate articles and reports on almost any topic they can think of.

Students of law and government have at their fingertips complete, searchable files of court decisions, laws, and the Congressional Record through the WESTLAW and BRS (Bibliographic Retrieval Systems) data sources.

None of these data bases instructs students directly, as do most of the other programs reviewed in this book. Rather, they are tools that social studies teachers or students can use to teach themselves. Students use them to complete assignments and projects; teachers use them to keep up with their fields and to gather ideas and information for lessons. In most cases, the teacher works in concert with the school librarian to access the off-site data bases; in fact, some schools already subscribe to one or more of them through the library.

Generally a school must purchase a subscription to the data-base service it wants to use and must then pay an additional on-line charge for each hour or minute of actual use. Subscriptions range from $10 to $500, depending partly on length of subscription, and hourly fees range from $5 to $200. Efficient users can search for and access data quickly, so that fees are measured in minutes instead of hours. Most social studies data bases cost less than $1 a minute to use. So the cost of using them is competitive with the price of a new set of textbooks or a magazine subscription for the class.

Logistical hurdles loom larger than financial ones in many schools, however. Most classrooms are not wired for telephone service; few school computers are equipped with the inexpensive modems that are needed to connect with the telephone; few librarians are familiar with electronic research; and the math teachers who often control the school's computers are not likely to be experts in this new use of the microcomputer. Also, the data bases are generally only half as expensive to use in the evenings and on weekends, when school is not in session.

A good place to begin the logistical arrangement is in the school library, where there is usually a telephone and often a computer. Another good place is at home, where you can learn the ropes of telecommunications in a more flexible and relaxed setting. Begin with the less expensive, more general services such as CompuServe; then graduate to the more comprehensive encyclopedic services such as DIALOG or the New York Times Information Service. Combine efforts with the school librarian as you seek funding and equipment for this kind of new resource for the school.

Off-site Data-base Services

The following examples illustrate how off-site data bases can be used in social studies teaching. The examples are neither exhaustive nor exemplary; they were chosen simply to provide a glimpse of what's available.

CompuServe. This service and its competitor, The Source, are used mostly for communications. Here we look at the data-base aspects of CompuServe, which is the less expensive of the two, costing $6 per evening hour but nothing for subscription. CompuServe is "menu-driven": The user selects choices from "menus" of topics that become increasingly detailed as the computer search continues. A sample session begins with a call to a local TELENET phone number. (TELENET is a long-distance data network that can connect you with CompuServe's Ohio-based computers for about $2 an hour.) When a user enters the CompuServe system by logging on (identifying himself or herself) with a user number and password, the user is presented with the "top menu," a list of the general topics available (see Figure 2.1).

Figure 2.1. *Top Menu for Compu-Serve.*

```
CompuServe                    TOP

 1 Instructions/User Information
 2 Find a Topic
 3 Communications/Bulletin Bds.
 4 News/Weather/Sports
 5 Travel
 6 The Electronic MALL/Shopping
 7 Money Matters/Markets
 8 Entertainment/Games
 9 Home/Health/Family
10 Reference/Education
11 Computers/Technology
12 Business/Other Interests

Enter choice number !
```

Reprinted by permission of CompuServe Incorporated.

No. 10 on the top menu, the "Reference/Education" category, contains the information most obviously useful for social studies. Choosing this option, we are offered another menu of choices (see Figure 2.2). Here we are faced with nine types of references. Avoiding choice no. 4, the interesting-looking but expensive "Information on Demand" (IOD) service (IOD is a private firm that conducts searches for $200 to $300 a shot), we go back to no. 2, the "U.S. Government Publications" file. Scanning through the available publications, we find one containing economic data that would be useful in tomorrow's class, and we have our printer make a copy of it on paper.

This search has not taken much time (about 5 minutes worth, or 30¢), so, finishing with the Reference section, we decide to catch up on the latest world and national news. Selecting the "News/Weather/Sports" option, we get ourselves to the Associated Press (AP) Videotex wire. Still further choices are presented on the AP wire: a news summary; weather; the national, world, or Washington, D.C., news in detail; political news; and several types of business news. A check with the "newsbrief" summary produces a rundown of the major stories of the moment, on this day ranging from government squabbles in Africa, to a hijacking in South America, to the latest medical marvels. The summary is updated hourly by AP.

This foray into CompuServe has lasted less than 10 minutes, at a total cost of less than $1 for both on-line computer charges and long-distance

Figure 2.2. *Submenu for Compu-Serve.*

```
CompuServe                REFERENCE

REFERENCE
  1 Academic Am. Encyclopedia ($)
  2 U.S. Government Publications
  3 Demographics ($E)
  4 Information on Demand ($)
  5 Naked Eye Astronomy
EDUCATION
  6 Services for Educators
  7 Services for the Handicapped/
    Students and Parents
  8 Forums
  9 Educational Games

Enter choice !
```

Reprinted by permission of Compuserve Incorporated.

telephone charges. While we did not locate anything that couldn't have been found in the local library or on the six o'clock evening news, we located it quickly, inexpensively, and without moving from the desk. Had we wished to spend more time with the CompuServe data bases, we could have viewed an educational software program in social studies or searched an encyclopedia. CompuServe is not the richest source of social studies data bases, but it is the least expensive and easiest to use for the beginner.

DIALOG. This service houses the richest collection: more than 200 data bases, 22 of them in the humanities and social sciences, 6 on news, 8 on government and law. Each data base is a separate collection of articles, citations, and information, but all are searchable by the same DIALOG search system. The following collections are of most interest to social studies teachers:

America: History and Life
Family Resources
Historical Abstracts
Middle East Index
PAIS (Public Administration Policy) International
Population Bibliography
Psychoinfo
Religion Index
Social Scisearch
Sociological Abstracts
U.S. Political Science Documents
World Affairs Report
Magazine Index
National Newspaper Index
Newsearch
UPI (United Press International) News
Washington Post Index
American Statistics Index
Congressional Record Abstracts
Federal Index
Laborlaw
Legal Resource Index
Criminal Justice

Most of these are indexes of journals and periodicals. They are used, like the printed *Reader's Guide to Periodical Literature,* to find the titles and locations of articles on a given subject. The electronic indexes have

two added features that distinguish them from the printed library resources: searchability and abstracts.

Each article or book that is put into the index is given a series of descriptors — words or phrases that denote what is covered in the article. For
example, a historical piece on Theodore Roosevelt's politics might be given
the descriptors "Progressive Era"; "populism"; "Roosevelt, Theodore"; and
so forth. A search of the data base keys into these descriptors, so that the
Roosevelt article would be brought up by a researcher who searched with
any of the key words just listed. In fact, DIALOG allows searches by combi-
nations of descriptors, making it possible to find those items that contain both *progressive* and *antitrust*, for instance, as key words. An ex-
perienced searcher can narrow down a selection of resources quickly and
accurately to access only those items that are truly useful.

The search cites articles for each item found: title, author, date, location, and length. Most searchers next wish to find out a little more about
some of the articles, so DIALOG data bases provide an abstract of each
one, giving a paragraph or two that summarizes the article and its find-
ings. Reading the abstracts gets the researcher valuable information and
helps him or her decide whether or not to get a copy of the entire article.
In most cases, the entire article is not in the DIALOG data base; one must
get the article from one's library or through interlibrary loan.

DIALOG contains the largest collection of information resources that
is publicly accessible by computer. The average cost for using the social
studies data bases just described is $67 an hour, or about $1 a minute.
A 10-minute, $10 search for every student is not within the reach of most
social studies budgets, so student use of DIALOG should be reserved for
special cases or large-group projects. This service is especially useful for
the teacher, who can rapidly gather information needed for planning
lessons that will benefit large numbers of students.

Other Data Bases.   Table 2.1 shows the social studies courses for which
CompuServe, DIALOG, the New York Times News Service, and the Dow
Jones News Service might be useful. Readers should recognize that many
of the data bases that are through DIALOG are also available through
Bibliographic Retrieval Systems (BRS) of Latham, New York. The Times
and the Dow Jones services are aimed at narrower interests and so are
limited to newspaper files and business files. But they are accessible and
searchable, just like the others, and can serve to enhance social studies
research and teaching.

The use of an off-site data base has the advantage of bringing into
the social studies classroom new kinds of information in a vastly more
immediate and efficient manner. As the amount of information that we

Table 2.1. *Data Bases Useful to the Social Studies.*

COURSE TITLE	DATA BASES

American History	America: History and Life (DIALOG)
	Historical Abstracts (DIALOG)
	Socialscisearch (DIALOG)
	Academic American Encyclopedia (BRS,
	    CompuServe, DIALOG)
	American Statistics Index (DIALOG)
	Newspaper files (DIALOG, NYTIS,
	    CompuServe, others)

World Studies	AP News Wire (CompuServe) UPI News (DIALOG) Newsearch (DIALOG) Middle East Index (DIALOG) Population Bibliography (DIALOG) Travel Information File (CompuServe)
Government and Law	PAIS International (DIALOG) Congressional Record Abstracts (DIALOG) Legal Resource Index (DIALOG) Federal Index (DIALOG) Various News Services (BRS, Compu Serve, NYTIS, DIALOG) Criminal Justice Periodical Index (DIALOG)
Sociology, Psychology	American Statistics Index (DIALOG) Family Resources (DIALOG) Psychinfo (DIALOG) Sociological Abstracts (DIALOG)
Economics	Dow Jones News Service (DJNS) Commodity News Service (The Source, CompuServe) Market Quotes (The Source, CompuServe, DJNS) Business Information Wire (CompuServe) Standard & Poor's Information File (CompuServe)
Current Events	New York Times Information Service (NYTIS) AP Videotex Wire (CompuServe) UPI News (The Source, DIALOG) Electronic Newspapers (NYTIS, The Source, CompuServe) Newsearch (DIALOG)

Note: BRS = Bibliographic Retrieval Service; NYTIS = New York Times Information Service; DJNS = Dow Jones News Service.

teach increases, these electronic searching and retrieval methods will turn from a luxury to a necessity. Neither the school library nor the individual social studies teacher will be able to keep on file and to organize all of the items needed for teaching.

Using these data bases also forces the student to learn how to find information: to narrow the topic, to use key descriptors, to separate the relevant from the irrelevant, and to design new schemes for organizing data. The researcher who learns these skills is rewarded with fast, accurate, and complete resources at the touch of a keyboard.

Although the price of these services has come down, they are still too expensive for daily use by students. But as more scholars make use of them and as more services compete in the market, the price will drop, so that on-line information retrieval will be part and parcel of public school education in social studies.

There is a disadvantage to all of this, however. Electronic searches, focusing on citations and abstracts alone, can tend to encourage shallow research that never consults original sources and seldom confronts raw data. And the student who learns to research solely by computer may not develop the skills of finding information in the library. Without the careful guidance of an informed teacher, these data bases are of little use to the social studies classroom. The data bases alone do not teach or inform; they are properly used as part of a well-planned lesson and research strategy.

☐   WORD PROCESSING   ☐

Many language arts teachers and English teachers have already discovered the advantages of having students use word processing programs both inside and outside of their classrooms. Besides producing papers that are easier to read because they are neater, students who learn to use word processors tend to write better papers. This is because the computer allows them to edit their work easily. The look of their neat and clean final product as it comes out of the printer also gives them a great psychological boost.

In the social studies, writing has become something of a lost art. Most textbook publishers do not even include essay questions in their texts or in the test packages designed to accompany the texts. We seem to be living in the age of the short-answer question. Research papers are still assigned, but it can be hard to get students to pay attention to their work on these occasional papers, given the many other demands on their time and attention.

Unfortunately, many high school graduates today arrive at college not knowing how to construct a good social studies essay or research paper. They may know the facts, but they don't know how to state their point of view and support it with logical arguments. What they need is practice, practice, practice!

How to Select a Word Processor

Access to a computer and word processor can make that practice much easier. With a word processor, students can quickly enter text into the computer. They can edit their work by moving text around to buttress their arguments. The text can be stored on a disk and retrieved later for a second look. Sections of text can also be cleanly and quickly deleted if the writers change their minds (and it won't make the final paper look messy). Students can also quickly search for certain key phrases or sections of text and go back to delete or add to them.

When the paper is finally done, printed out, and handed in, it is also much easier to hand it back and ask for extensive rewriting, since the text is stored in a form that can easily be reworked. This rewrite process is essential to learning what makes a good paper and how to edit one's own work.

Every good word processor should have the attributes just described. Some other questions to ask in selecting a word processing system are:

How much memory does it have? How long a term paper can it store?
How many commands are there for editing the text? For example, how can you move around parts of the text? Do you move word by word, sentence by sentence, paragraph by paragraph or in all three ways?
Can you restore what you have deleted?
Can you merge different files from the disk together? In other words, can you combine specified parts of one document and put them with another?
When printing the text out, does it allow you to set the margins, set the number of spaces between lines, number the pages, and otherwise format your writing?
And—a useful feature for taking surveys, writing for information, and so forth: Does it do format letters?

Three word processing programs that have all of these abilities are BANK STREET WRITER, APPLE WRITER, and HOMEWORD. These programs have differences that you should consider, when selecting one, in terms of your students' particular needs. BANK STREET WRITER, for instance, is useful for younger children. It uses large letters, easy-to-remember commands, and puts a border around the text to make it easy to define.

APPLE WRITER is the most complicated of the three programs in terms of commands to remember, but compared to many other programs on the market it is simple. It is intended to be an easy-to-use but still sophisticated product. Some special features it includes are a split screen that allows you to see different parts of the document at once, and the ability to save your own glossary of often-used words that can be easily inserted into the text.

HOMEWORD uses icons (pictorial symbols) as part of a command menu that appears at the bottom of the computer screen. You select what you want to do by moving to the icon (which is labeled) with the arrow keys on the keyboard. It has fewer commands than APPLE WRITER, because when you select an icon you are asked detailed questions or given directions, so that you don't have to remember all the commands. For example, if you select the icon for moving text from one place to another, a direction that appears at the bottom of the screen then gives you instructions, such as "Move the cursor to the beginning of the text." (The cursor shows the point at which you are currently entering text.)

Again, the computer is not going to replace the guidance that a student needs from a teacher on how to construct a good paper, but it can assist in the process. Perhaps someday down the road, students won't hand in papers. Instead they will hand in disks with their papers stored on them. With some additional software, these papers will be edited, commented upon, and graded by the teacher right on the disk, saving a lot of time — and trees.

☐   STATISTICAL ANALYSIS AND GRAPHING   ☐

The largest-selling computer software programs are electronic spreadsheets — programs that allow the user to enter numbers into the computer, manipulate the numbers in various ways, and then produce tables, graphs, and statistical summaries of what the numbers mean. In business, especially, this kind of software is obviously quite valuable and thus is widely used. We can use these same well-developed and efficient tools in teaching social studies.

Educational Value

The graphics and statistical programs described in this section do not teach social studies directly. Like the data-base and filing programs discussed earlier in this chapter, these programs are simply tools that teachers (and students) can use to make sense out of the wealth of information that the social studies deal with. These graphics and statistical programs are not peculiar to the social studies; they can serve a similar purpose in the math or science class.

Computers are great with numbers. But the teacher cannot simply enter numerical data into the computer and expect to get meaningful information out. The computer needs detailed instructions on what to do with the numbers and on how to present the results. Graphics and statistical programs provide a large set of ready-made instructions and also allow you to create your own special instructions for the computer. The programs set up the screen like a blank page upon which you write the numbers you want to deal with; they allow you to manipulate these numbers with simple statistical tools; they then allow you to see the results in a variety of ways.

Because these programs have such wide use in business, they are today quite well developed, efficient, and easy to use. Business people use them to store information on such things as sales, inventory, and prices; to examine and project trends and relationships; to prove that one factor is affecting another; and finally to present quantitative data in an informative visual mode. The designers and producers of this kind of software are in spirited competition with one another, and so the quality and capability of the products is increasing as their prices are dropping. They are becoming easy for the computer novice to use along the way. This application of the microcomputer is ready for us in the social studies.

Unlike the drill-and-practice, tutorial, and simulation programs discussed earlier, these graphics and statistical programs can use different data each time the program is run. A single purchase by the social studies department will probably be sufficient for everyone's use for several years. As you use these powerful programs and become familiar with their capabilities, you will think of new ways to employ them in your work, and new sets of numbers will find their way in. These are truly versatile tools.

Three types of programs are included in this discussion: electronic spreadsheets that deal with rows and columns of numbers; data-base programs that allow for statistical manipulation; and graphics packages that can turn numbers into graphs. We will look closely at LOTUS 1-2-3, a spreadsheet that is the top-selling piece of business software today; DATA-BASE, JR., a data-base program for young students that performs some statistical functions; and PFS:GRAPH, a popular graphics program. These three were chosen because they are widely available (the chances are good that your school already owns at least one of them); they are published in several versions, so that they can be used on the various brands of microcomputers; and they are very easy to use. In addition, the last two are quite inexpensive.

Spreadsheet Programs

LOTUS 1-2-3.   The versatility of LOTUS 1-2-3 has made it the top seller
in its field. It can do for numbers what a word processor can do for words.
Its designers have anticipated all the things you might possibly want to
do with rows and columns of numbers and made it very easy for you to
do them.

LOTUS 1-2-3 is an electronic spreadsheet. It turns the computer screen
into a blank page with rows and columns on it. You fill the rows and
columns with words and numbers: whatever words and numbers you
wish, organized on the page as you desire. In certain rows and columns,
you can enter formulas that tell the computer to add, multiply, or perform statistical functions on the numbers and can see the final results
displayed on the screen. Finally, you can instruct the machine to print
the spreadsheet onto paper or turn it into a graph, which can also be
viewed on the screen or printed out.

To show you how LOTUS 1-2-3 works, let's examine a very simple example from the social studies. Table 2.2 shows how a social studies
teacher has entered information on 15 of the states into the LOTUS 1-2-3
spreadsheet. She simply typed in the name of the state, its population,
and its area in square miles into three columns on the spreadsheet.

She did not have to add them all up to get the totals and averages,
though. The program allowed her to put a formula in the TOTAL row that
automatically instructed the computer to add up the numbers in the column above and place the result in the TOTAL row. A similar formula
computed the averages. All the teacher had to do was to state the formula: @SUM(B3...B17). She did not need to know computer programming.

Now that the data is in the spreadsheet, we can manipulate it. We
can tell LOTUS 1-2-3 to SORT the list by size of population (from highest to
lowest), and within seconds we see a new list on the screen (see Table 2.3).

Similarly, we can sort it by geographic area or even alphabetically by
state. Using the graphics function of LOTUS 1-2-3, we can also see this
same information in a variety of visual modes: a pie graph, scatter dia-
gram, or bar graph. This sorting and graphing is done with a few keystrokes; no programming is necessary.

Now let's suppose we want to derive some new information from our
data on the 15 states. We want to figure the population density of each
state: that is, the number of people per square mile. The spreadsheet
allows us to create a new column, "Population per Square Mile," that will
compute this for us (see Table 2.4). Again, the teacher only needed to
type in the column heading and enter a simple formula: (B2/C2) (i.e., population divided by area), to get the desired result. We have the informa-

Table 2.2. Information on 15 States (from LOTUS 1-2-3).

STATE	POPULATION	AREA (SQUARE MILES)
Delaware	548,104	2,057
Pennsylvania	11,793,909	45,333
New Jersey	7,168,164	7,836
Georgia	4,589,575	58,876
Connecticut	3,032,217	5,009
Massachusetts	5,689,170	8,257
Maryland	3,922,399	10,577
South Carolina	2,590,516	31,055
New Hampshire	737,681	9,304
Virginia	4,648,494	40,817
New York	18,190,740	49,576
North Carolina	5,082,059	52,586
Rhode Island	949,723	1,214
Vermont	444,732	9,609
Kentucky	3,219,311	40,395
TOTAL	72,606,794	372,501
AVERAGE	4,840,453	24,833

tion we need in seconds; we could next sort the list again, this time in order of population density, or present the densities in graphic form.

A spreadsheet program such as LOTUS 1-2-3 allows social studies teachers and students to store data, manipulate it, project from it, and show it in a variety of ways. From the results you get, you or the students may be better able to draw conclusions or derive meaning. It can help you to see the numbers in different ways, so that they might make more sense to you.

Applications
Our example of the 15 states is a simple one. How else might a spreadsheet program be put to work in the social studies classroom?

Instead of states, we could do the same thing with towns, counties, or countries of the world. Most spreadsheets have enough room for several hundred rows.

Table 2.3. *Information on 15 States, Sorted by Population (from LOTUS 1-2-3).*

STATE	POPULATION	AREA (SQUARE MILES)
New York	18,190,740	49,576
Pennsylvania	11,793,909	45,333
New Jersey	7,168,164	7,836
Massachusetts	5,689,170	8,257
North Carolina	5,082,059	52,586
Virginia	4,648,494	40,817
Georgia	4,589,575	58,876
Maryland	3,922,399	10,577
Kentucky	3,219,311	40,395
Connecticut	3,032,217	5,009
South Carolina	2,590,516	31,055
Rhode Island	949,723	1,214
New Hampshire	737,681	9,304
Delaware	548,104	2,057
Vermont	444,732	9,609
TOTAL	72,606,794	372,501
AVERAGE	4,840,453	24,833

To look at historical trends, we could let each column of the spreadsheet represent a given year or decade. The graphing possibilities
of such a spreadsheet can be quite useful.

Each president of the United States or each signer of the Declara-
tion of Independence could occupy one row of the spreadsheet.
The columns could contain the person's date of birth, years in
office, number of children, party, home state, and other personal
data. Most spreadsheets can mix numerical and verbal data and
manipulate both.

Your own data—on students, classes, groups—can be entered into the
spreadsheet for later manipulation and analysis. Questionnaire
data is especially amenable to storage on a spreadsheet.

Both teachers and students can use the spreadsheet program. Teachers can use it to help them prepare presentations; students can include
information gleaned from the spreadsheet in their reports.

Using spreadsheets in the social studies has several benefits. It allows us, as we have never been well able to do before, to show quantitative data — numbers — in dramatic and visual ways, without the burden of extensive calculation and plotting. Spreadsheets can allow us to bring more quantitative data into our teaching and thus get closer to original sources.

Programs such as LOTUS 1-2-3 allows us and our students to use numerical data to prove a point. With instant, professional-looking graphs and tables, we will be less afraid to use quantitative data and more inclined to let students draw their own conclusions from raw data. These programs encourage a social science approach in the classroom and make numbers more easily accessible to students.

Selecting a Spreadsheet Program

The chances are good that your school already owns a spreadsheet program. Check with the business department, the math department, or the computer lab. Since you will use it only periodically, you need not

Table 2.4. *Information on 15 States, with Population per Square Mile Added (from LOTUS 1-2-3).*

STATE	POPULATION	AREA/SQ. MILES	POP/SQ. MILES
New Jersey	7,168,164	7,836	915
Rhode Island	949,723	1,214	782
Massachusetts	5,689,170	8,257	689
Connecticut	3,032,217	5,009	605
Maryland	3,922,399	10,577	371
New York	18,190,740	49,576	367
Delaware	548,104	2,057	266
Pennsylvania	11,793,909	45,333	260
Virginia	4,648,494	40,817	114
North Carolina	5,082,059	52,586	97
South Carolina	2,590,516	31,055	83
Kentucky	3,219,311	40,395	80
New Hampshire	737,681	9,304	79
Georgia	4,589,575	58,876	78
Vermont	444,732	9,609	46
TOTAL	72,606,794	372,501	195
AVERAGE	4,840,453	24,833	322

have the software in your possession all the time. A full-powered spreadsheet such as LOTUS 1-2-3 costs about $400 and runs only on IBM-PC computers. Simpler spreadsheets such as VISICALC and MULTIPLAN sell for less than $150 and are available for Apple, Radio Shack, and Commodore computers. They cannot make all the graphs that LOTUS can, they are limited to 250 rows of data, and they lack some of the advanced statistical functions. Still less expensive is SPREADSHEET, JR. from Intellectual Software; it is designed for students in the middle grades and spreadsheet beginners. The table of data on the states, printed out from SPREADSHEET, JR., is shown in Table 2.5.

Whichever spreadsheet you choose, it is best to use it first for simple projects, then tackle larger sets of data as you become more familiar with its power. This discussion has only touched the surface of what a spreadsheet program can do for the social studies; additional functions such as regression analysis and statistical work can take us even further into social studies data analysis.

Graphics Programs

PFS:GRAPH.   Some computer programs are designed simply to turn numerical data into graphs. PFS:GRAPH, sister to the PFS:FILE data base discussed earlier, can make bar, line, or pie graphs from social studies data. It cannot statistically manipulate the data; it simply turns numbers into pictures. PFS:GRAPH is easy to use and is available for almost every brand of microcomputer.

Table 2.5. Printout of Data on 15 States (from SPREADSHEET, JR.).

A	STATE	POPULATION	AREA	REPS (IN CONGRESS)	PEOPLE/SQ MI
B					
C	DELAWARE	548,104	2,057	1	266
D	PENNSYLVANIA	11,793,909	45,333	25	260
E	NEW JERSEY	7,168,164	7,836	15	914
F	GEORGIA	4,589,575	58,876	10	77
G	CONNECTICUT	3,032,217	5,009	6	605
H	MASSACHUSETTS	5,689,170	8,257	12	689
I	MARYLAND	3,922,399	10,577	8	370
J	SOUTH CAROLINA	2,590,516	31,055	6	83
K	NEW HAMPSHIRE	737,681	9,304	2	79
L	VIRGINIA	4,648,494	40,817	10	113
M	NEW YORK	18,190,740	49,575	39	366
N	NORTH CAROLINA	5,082,059	52,586	11	96
O	RHODE ISLAND	949,723	1,214	2	782
P	VERMONT	444,732	9,609	1	46
Q	KENTUCKY	3,219,311	40,395	7	79
R					
S	TOTAL	72,606,794	372,501	155	4,825
T	AVERAGE	4,840,452	24,833	10	321

We could take data from some of the same 15 states that we used in our LOTUS 1-2-3 example (Tables 2.2–2.4) to illustrate the functions of PFS:GRAPH. Once we have entered the data into the PFS program, we can choose one of several different types of graphs to display it on. The examples shown in Figure 2.3, two bar graphs and one pie chart, were all produced automatically by the computer and printed out on a standard dot-matrix printer. It took only a few minutes to define the graph and get the final output.

Applications

Certainly more complex examples than these could be graphed to help teach various social studies concepts. Often a graph can show a relationship among factors that is not easily grasped by looking at a table of numbers or statistics. In these circumstances, graph-making programs like this can be quite valuable to the social studies teacher or student. Here are some examples:

Towns, nations, and countries can take the place of states in our example. Relationships among the data can be shown in a variety of ways as different types of graphs represent the same data.
We can enter data for successive periods in history and use PFS:GRAPH to show trends over time in an effective visual manner. For example, Figure 2.4 shows two different examples of graphs concerning trends in Vermont agriculture between 1840 and 1980.
Data from questionnaires and surveys can quickly be turned into graphs that show the results.
Elections can be analyzed in new ways: Once the vote totals from the various districts are entered into the computer, a variety of comparisons can be presented instantly as graphs.
Data from an almanac, Census Bureau reports, historical records, news reports, and textbooks can be turned into useful graphs by both teacher and student.

Computer graphics packages can produce illustrations for student reports and presentations; help the teacher prepare a graphic transparency or handout in seconds instead of hours; and provide stimuli for test questions (graphs are used widely in the Scholastic Aptitude Test and other standardized tests). A computer graph can help to make a point in a debate or oral presentation by students, since many concepts from the social sciences are best taught by means of graphs. Graphics packages are versatile tools that will find more and more uses at the hands of the creative social studies teacher.

(*Continued on page 66*)

Figure 2.3. *Bar Graphs and Pie Chart Produced by* PFS:GRAPH *Showing State Populations, State Areas, and State Populations as Percentages.*

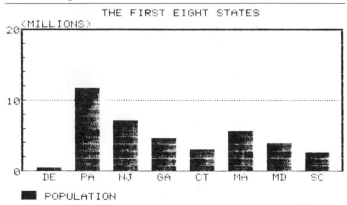

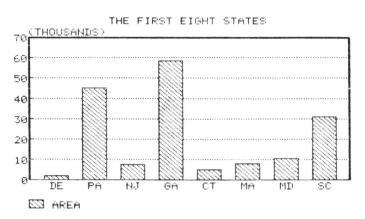

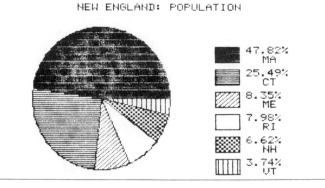

Figure 2.4. *Line Graphs Produced by* PFS:GRAPH *Showing Agricultural Trends in Vermont.*

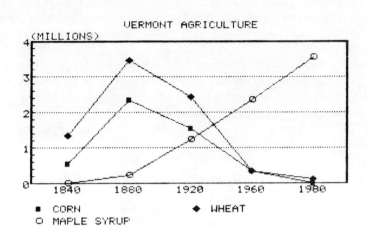

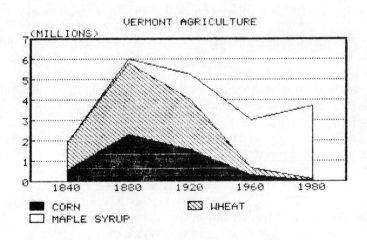

Using graphs is an especially effective way to get students to draw their own conclusions from data. Often the numbers alone do not possess the power to show what's happening; the same data, presented as a graph, can allow more of your students to draw the desired conclusion.

Before computers and graphics packages were available, a simple graph like the ones just discussed would have taken almost an hour to plan and construct, so using graphs in our teaching was a rare occurrence. With this new capability, we can use graphs more frequently and with more types of lessons.

Your school may already own PFS:GRAPH or a similar graphics package. Or, since this program can serve a useful purpose for science and math courses, it may be possible to share the cost ($100 to $150) of a good graphics package. PFS:GRAPH is available in versions for just about all of the popular microcomputers, so it should not be difficult for you to make use of it in your school.

Data-base Programs with Statistical and Graphics Capability

DATABASE, JR.   Some data-base programs allow the user to perform statistical manipulations of the stored data and to graph the data as well. DATABASE, JR. is an inexpensive program of this type that was specially designed for students. With this program and others like it, even students in the middle grades (and their teachers) can construct their own data bases and do some elementary statistical analysis and graphing with the data.

A data-base program allows you to enter, store, and organize data and then to get it out in various ways. DATABASE, JR. provides a 50-by-50–item matrix to store data in; that is, the user can name up to 50 items (each state in the United States might be one item) and up to 50 categories (area, population, and state capitals are examples of categories) as he or she sets up a data base. The program then asks the user to enter the data that is needed to fill the data base: For example, it asks for "FLORIDA AREA?" and waits for you to enter the proper number, and so forth. When your data base is full, the program automatically stores it on the disk.

A menu of six choices, shown in Figure 2.5, then allows you to take the next step. Choosing to GET INFORMATION OUT, you are faced with several choices that involve statistical analysis (see Figure 2.6). You can FIGURE TOTALS AND AVERAGES, COUNT DATA, or SORT.

As an example, we have created a data base with several bits of information on each of the states. We can quickly compute that the average area of the states is 72,301 square miles (and in doing so see that the total area of the country is 3,615,047 square miles). It took the computer less than a second to produce this result.

Figure 2.5. Main Menu for
DATABASE, JR.

---

1. START NEW DATA BASE

2. GET DATA BASE FROM DISK

3. PUT INFORMATION IN

4. GET INFORMATION OUT

5. MAKE-A-GRAPH

6. ERASE A FILE FROM DISK

"STATES" DATA BASE NOW IN MEMORY.

DATABASE, JR., copyright 1984 by J. G.
Lengel.

Next, by selecting the COUNT DATA option, we can find all the states that are larger than average and see them listed on paper. Or we could sort the states in order of population (from lowest to highest), and in no time at all get a list that looks like the one in Table 2.6.

In a similar fashion, DATABASE, JR. allows the student to print a list of all the states that are smaller (or larger) than his or her own, or to sort them by area, or to examine all the data for a particular state.

This program also has an integrated graphing routine. Any of the categories can be displayed on the computer screen as a simple bar graph and can then be printed out on paper if desired. Figure 2.7 is part of a bar graph produced by DATABASE, JR. from this same data base of the populations of the states.

(*Continued on page 70*)

Figure 2.6. "Get Information Out"
Menu for DATABASE, JR.

---

1. LIST ALL DATA

2. LIST ONE DATUM

3. FIGURE TOTALS AND AVERAGES

4. COUNT DATA

5. LIST ONE ITEM

6. SEARCH FOR KEY WORD

7. DOUBLE SEARCH

8. SORT

DATABASE, JR., copyright 1984 by J. G.
Lengel.

***Table* 2.6.** *States Sorted by Population (from* DATABASE, JR.*).*

ALASKA:	302,173
WYOMING:	332,416
VERMONT:	444,732
NEVADA:	488,738
DELAWARE:	548,104
NORTH DAKOTA:	617,761
SOUTH DAKOTA:	666,257
MONTANA:	694,409
IDAHO:	713,008
NEW HAMPSHIRE:	737,681
HAWAII:	769,913
RHODE ISLAND:	949,723
MAINE:	993,663
NEW MEXICO:	1,016,000
UTAH:	1,059,273
NEBRASKA:	1,483,791
WEST VIRGINIA:	1,744,237
ARIZONA:	1,772,482
ARKANSAS:	1,923,295
OREGON:	2,091,385
COLORADO:	2,207,259
MISSISSIPPI:	2,216,912
KANSAS:	2,249,071
OKLAHOMA:	2,559,253
SOUTH CAROLINA:	2,590,516
IOWA:	2,825,041
CONNECTICUT:	3,032,217
KENTUCKY:	3,219,311
WASHINGTON:	3,409,169
ALABAMA:	3,444,165
LOUISIANA:	3,643,180
MINNESOTA:	3,805,069
MARYLAND:	3,922,399
TENNESSEE:	3,924,164
WISCONSIN:	4,417,933
GEORGIA:	4,589,575
VIRGINIA:	4,648,494
MISSOURI:	4,677,399
NORTH CAROLINA:	5,082,059
INDIANA:	5,193,669
MASSACHUSETTS:	5,689,170
FLORIDA:	6,789,443
NEW JERSEY:	7,168,164
MICHIGAN:	8,875,083
OHIO:	10,652,017
ILLINOIS:	11,113,976
TEXAS:	11,196,730
PENNSYLVANIA:	11,793,909
NEW YORK:	18,190,740
CALIFORNIA:	19,953,134

SEARCH COMPLETE.

Figure 2.7. *Bar Graph of State Populations Produced*
by DATABASE, JR.

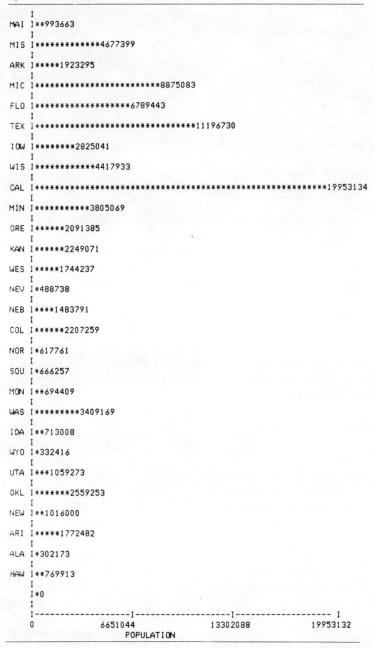

```
       I
 MAI   I**993663
       I
 MIS   I*************4677399
       I
 ARK   I******1923295
       I
 MIC   I*************************8875083
       I
 FLO   I********************6789443
       I
 TEX   I**********************************11196730
       I
 IOW   I*********2825041
       I
 WIS   I*************4417933
       I
 CAL   I**********************************************************************19953134
       I
 MIN   I***********3805069
       I
 ORE   I******2091385
       I
 KAN   I******2249071
       I
 WES   I*****1744237
       I
 NEV   I*488738
       I
 NEB   I****1483791
       I
 COL   I******2207259
       I
 NOR   I*617761
       I
 SOU   I*666257
       I
 MON   I**694409
       I
 WAS   I*********3409169
       I
 IDA   I**713008
       I
 WYO   I*332416
       I
 UTA   I***1059273
       I
 OKL   I*******2559253
       I
 NEW   I**1016000
       I
 ARI   I*****1772482
       I
 ALA   I*302173
       I
 HAW   I**769913
       I
       I*0
       I
       I-------------------I-------------------I-------------------I
       0          6651044            13302088            19953132
                         POPULATION
```

69

Computers and software such as DATABASE, JR. allow you to design and create your own (or your student's own) collections of information and then help you to see relationships among the data quickly and easily. Any kind of data can be collected and organized: statistics concerning states, countries, or towns; questionnaire results; information on the president or world leaders; economic indicators for various months, years, or decades. The software is simple enough to be used immediately by teachers and student alike. And at one-tenth the cost of LOTUS 1-2-3, or of more powerful and complex data bases such as dBASE II, DATABASE, JR. may be a good place for the beginner to start.

The Future of Statistical and Graphics Packages

Each new year will bring us more powerful and easier-to-use products that permit the manipulation and presentation of data. Competition will bring the prices within reach of our materials budgets and will encourage the development of greater software capability.

We will also see the marketing of data bases and statistical packages with data already in them: census data, almanac data, economic data, and so forth (see the "Guide to Resources" in the appendix for an example). You will not need to construct your own collections. The use of a computerized data base will become a common skill among office workers and educators, and data bases will become a common tool for the student to use in school.

But already today the resources are available for the social studies teacher to make spreadsheets, graphing, and statistical work a part of everyday teaching and learning.

☐   CLASSROOM MANAGEMENT   ☐

For many social studies teachers, their first contact with computers in school is not as a help with instruction but as a record-keeping and management device. Most schools today have computerized the keeping of certain student records, and many faculties have put the computer to good use in keeping track of grades and assignments. To the high school social studies teacher with a load of 150 or more students, this help with paperwork can turn the computer into a godsend.

As we have learned already in this chapter, the computer is a marvel at storing and keeping track of information. In this section, we will examine how computers can be used to store and figure grades and test averages, construct tests and assignment sheets, and administer pre- and post-tests to students.

Computerize Your Gradebook

Ever since paper was invented, teachers have kept gradebooks. Usually green in color, these books contain pages and pages of little squares and places for student names. When students complete assignments or earn a grade on a test or a quiz, a record is entered into the appropriate box. When all grades are in, the teacher may use the grade book to set a "curve" to the scores. At the end of the marking period, a given student's grades will be totaled, averaged, and weighted so that a final grade can be assigned.

The computer can do this at least as well as you can. Programs now on the market provide for all the above-mentioned functions, and more. The hours previously spent with pencil and calculator can be turned into minutes. Results can be printed out in a class roster, an individual student report, or a section-by-section summary. These grade-keeping programs turn the computer's memory into the rows and columns and little boxes of the gradebook; have preprogrammed formulas for computing totals, averages, and curves; and have routines to generate common types of reports. Although none are designed specifically for the social studies, most are general enough for social studies teachers to make use of.

Before using the disk, you must set it up for your classes. You enter student names (and sometimes other information) according to sections and subjects, just as you would have entered them into the left-hand column of the green gradebook. These names are saved on the disk, so you never have to enter them again.

When it is time to record the scores from a test or assignment, the program will query you for the name and date of the test or assignment and then query you for the score of each student in turn. When all scores have been entered, the information is saved on the disk. At this point, the teacher usually has the option of figuring a class average and, if desired, putting the raw scores on some kind of a curve. The more sophisticated grade-keeping programs allow for several different types of curves. The option of printing out a class roster listing grades is also usually allowed at this point.

As the school year proceeds, and more and more scores and grades are entered, the programs can produce a "running average" for each student. This can be valuable information for the student as well as the teacher. Many of the programs can also print out the whole set of records—that is, provide you with a printed copy that looks just like the gradebook itself. Most teachers produce such a printout for the security it provides in case the disk should accidentally be erased.

The end of the marking period brings out the magic of the grade-keeping program. Student averages are computed in seconds; again, curves can be fitted to these data as well (for example, 10 percent A's, 30 percent B's, 30 percent C's, and so forth), and often a short report can be printed for each student, showing the assignments and the grades received.

In most cases, a single grade-keeping disk can serve an entire social studies department, with each teacher keeping his or her own data disk. These programs are available for most of the different microcomputers. And in many schools, the computer programming class has already prepared such a program for use by the school's teachers. Some of the more creative and sophisticated grade-keeping software has arisen from this source.

Test-making Software

The construction of tests and quizzes is part of the art of teaching the social studies. The choosing of topics, the wording of questions, the listing of possible right answers, provokes our thinking and shapes our teaching. So we often save our best tests for use year after year. A locked file drawer of ditto masters for tests is a common fixture in the social studies classroom.

Test-making software can help us with the design and storage of tests and quizzes. There are two general types: those that contain hundreds or thousands of already constructed test items; and those that allow the teacher to enter, store, and retrieve his or her own favorite questions. Both types allow for questions and items to be selected by the teacher, arranged into a test, and printed onto plain paper or onto a ditto master. Both essay questions and multiple-choice questions can be used, but the latter is more prevalent in the current range of software.

Once a bank of test questions is created, either by the teacher or by the publisher of the software, you can select the questions you desire for a given test. They can be selected from the current chapter in the textbook, the current unit, the semester course, or from all of the material covered during the year. The more questions in the bank, the more choices you have in constructing your test. Along with the printout of the test itself, the teacher can usually get a printed answer key to use in correcting the tests.

These programs are simply storage and retrieval devices; they do not design the questions or give the test for you. But they can make your work more efficient by handling paperwork and by allowing a wider choice of test items. A wide variety of open test-making software is available, and a few already designed social studies question banks are now on the market.

The Computer as Test Giver

With the wider availability of computers in labs, classrooms, and libraries, they can now be used to administer tests directly to students. The computer presents questions for the student to answer, keeps track of the score, and records the class results for the teacher. An experimental program for OMEGA LEARN provides an interesting example of this approach to class management.

OMEGA LEARN. The OMEGA LEARN program contains a bank of concepts and factual information about the Jacksonian period of American history, material normally covered in Unit 3 of the standard eleventh-grade American history text. Students begin their study of this unit by taking a computer pretest: Each one sits down at the keyboard and is presented with a series of questions that deal with the material covered in that unit.

But no two students get the same questions. The secret of the program is its ability to generate questions from the material in its information bank. Information is randomly selected from the bank, and the machine constructs a multiple-choice question out of it. Not even the teacher knows what the question will be. Figure 2.8 shows two examples of such randomly generated questions.

The student selects what he or she thinks is the correct answer, and the score is recorded. Then another question is constructed by the machine, and so forth. The student never gets the same question twice, and no two students get exactly the same test. But the information bank is constructed so that the questions are of approximately equal difficulty, and by selecting the information randomly any such differences are canceled out among students. When all the students have taken the pretest, the teacher gets a printout of the class results. These results can help determine the type and amount of teaching that needs to be done with this unit.

At the completion of the unit, the procedure is repeated as a post-test. Again, the questions deal with the same information but are asked in different ways. Post-test results for each member of the class are recorded, so that the teacher can see the relative progress of each student and perhaps assign a grade based on the difference between pre- and post-test scores.

The OMEGA LEARN system has another feature: The information bank can be searched like a data base by the student. In this way, the question format can be turned into an instructional device. If the student does not know the answer, he or she can search the data base and gather information on the topic in question and then select an answer.

Figure 2.8. *Sample Questions from* OMEGA LEARN.

In the removal of Indians from the Southeastern U.S., what did the
Cherokee Indians do?

1. Opposed the admission of California as a free state

2. Persuaded President Jackson to reduce federal government support
    for internal improvements such as the building of roads

3. Adopted a constitution making them dependents of the United States
    who were not subject to state laws

4. Developed the system of interchangeable parts

Select 1, 2, 3, or 4 or press D to search databases: ?

Andrew Jackson expressed his opposition to the rapid development of
the American economy in what situation?

1. Compromise of 1850

2. War with Mexico

3. War on the second Bank of the United States

4. Election of John Quincy Adams in 1824

Select 1, 2, 3, or 4 or press D to search databases: ?

Reprinted, by permission, from experimental material developed by Omega Learning Systems.

The machine-generated question (and possible right answers) are all
in plain English. They look as though they were written by human be-
ings. They make sense, but they're often surprising. Teachers observing
the results often comment that they've never thought about asking that
question in that way. The program can help us find new ways of looking
at the same familiar information that we're teaching.

☐   AUTHORING SYSTEMS   ☐

Some of the best social studies teaching happens not with commercially
prepared materials but with lessons and readings of the teacher's own

making. Can this same phenomenon occur with computers? How can the social studies teacher design and construct his or her own computer lessons?

The teacher could, of course, learn to program the computer and construct lessons from scratch, as the commercial software publishers do. Some social studies teachers have done this, with some success. But the time it takes to learn to program well enough to produce even a simple interactive lesson is beyond the limits of most teachers. A more feasible approach is to work with students in the school's computer programming courses, who can take the teacher's ideas and program them into lessons. This has met with great success in many high schools and can provide a continuing supply of home-grown products that meet the particular curricular needs of the teacher.

There is a third approach for the teacher who wants to create computer lessons but chooses not to learn computer programming. On the market today are several "authoring systems" or "authoring languages" that allow the nonprogrammer to create simple lessons.

These systems provide a preprogrammed "shell" into which the teacher types the materials for the lesson. For the most part, the "author" is restricted to text presentations, multiple-choice questions, and fill-in-the-blank formats. By using the system, the teacher can present questions and short readings of his or her own design, ask the questions that are the most important to his or her students, and look for the answers that he or she has been trying to teach. A limited authoring system for the Apple or TRS-80 computer costs less than $150, can be used by several departments in a school, and is probably a good investment. It takes only a few hours to learn the system well enough to produce a simple and short lesson.

More complex authoring systems are also available, notably for the Apple and IBM-PC lines of microcomputers. These allow you to create color graphics on the screen as well as text; to present questions in a variety of ways; and to "branch" to a new module, depending on the student's progress. The best of these can cost over $1,000 and require a considerable investment of time in order to use them fully. But this investment of time is still far less than that required to master BASIC or Pascal well enough to produce lessons of similar quality.

The chief limitation of the authoring systems now on the market is their restriction to text-based drill-and-practice lessons. Few of the systems provide complete branching; fewer still allow for any data base or reference-bank functions. Maps, tables, or graphs are often difficult if not impossible to include in the lessons, and free-form responses in plain English by the student are almost never allowed, except in the most expensive systems. And with the plethora of drill-and-practice software available from commercial publishers, often at less than $50 a disk and in most cases better than what can be produced with a simple authoring system, it may not be necessary to produce your own.

But for the teacher who does not find what he or she needs in the marketplace, an authoring system may be the best answer. Look for one that allows several forms of presenting information and for asking questions. Avoid those that restrict you to multiple-choice questions. Find out if the system has the capability to present graphs, tables, and maps, as well as text. Check out how much branching the system allows in structuring a lesson and how much interaction it fosters with the student. Finally, determine how easy it will be for you to use. Some authoring systems have more commands and codes to learn than does the BASIC programming language.

Educational authoring systems are marketed by all of the major microcomputer manufacturers and by scores of independent programmers. You will find them in the larger computer stores and in the various catalogs and periodicals about computers. The resource list at the end of this book contains a few of these authoring systems.

□3□
Extensions of the Computer

Chapter 2 discussed a number of applications of computers in social studies teaching. For all but one of these applications, the only equipment needed is a computer, including a disk drive and a disk. The other application — off-site data bases — reaches out past the immediate location of the computer and communicates in some way with the outside world.

There was a time in the brief history of microcomputers when almost every job done by the computer was self-contained; that is, all you needed was the computer and the software you wanted to run on it. Much can still be accomplished with a computer alone, but lately many extensions to the computer have come onto the market, and this trend is likely to continue.

By "extensions," we are referring to the connection of other equipment to your computer to enhance its capabilities. First, there is a large set of peripheral computer equipment (or "peripherals"), such as light pens and graphics tablets, that can add greatly to the computer's abilities. These are connected to the inside of your computer. The videodisk, which allows rapid access to thousands of frames of visual images, also has important computer applications and educational potential. Second, with other devices such as modems you can extend the reach of your computer beyond the confines of your immediate location, communicating with other computers, computer users, and data bases far away. Finally, new technology that links computers with other media such as television has created entirely new possibilities for communication, with important implications for society.

In this chapter we will describe some of the many and rapidly developing ways in which the computer can be interfaced, or connected electronically with other devices. Our intention is not to supply a wealth of technical details about the devices but rather to introduce you to what is out there and what you can do with it. For social studies teachers, there are several good reasons for knowing about these recent technical developments.

In the first place, everything we describe exists right now; it is part

77

of the world about which teachers should keep themselves informed. These days, it is likely that many students will know about computer-related developments before their teachers. There are many times more microcomputers in homes than in schools, and this trend is apparently increasing. Teachers should at least be informed.

Second, as the scenarios in Chapter 1 revealed, students in schools and homes are using these developments for learning—not necessarily in overwhelming, but in increasing, numbers. At least some of these techniques will probably become a standard part of school technology. Teachers should have a voice in making decisions about what schools need, and to do this they must have a base of knowledge.

Third, social studies teachers have a particular reason for keeping abreast of changes that are likely to affect our society. The domain of social studies is not only geography and history; an important role is to assess what is happening in the present and help students to make sense of it. New technologies are important not only as tools in the classroom but as subject matter for the social studies. Their use may have an effect on important political issues such as the right to privacy and access to information (discussed further in Chapter 4). If teachers are to help students to understand these issues, they need to be familiar with the technology behind them.

☐   PERIPHERAL COMPUTER EQUIPMENT   ☐

A *peripheral* is a piece of equipment that can be interfaced with a computer but is not essential for its operation. A functioning computer system, as you will remember from Chapter 1, needs input, output, a processing unit, and a primary storage area inside the computer, with secondary memory (usually a disk or tape) for permanent storage.

Input is usually entered with a keyboard that comes with the microcomputer, and output is usually produced on a screen that is connected to it by wires, or on a printer. Many devices have been developed to enhance or vary input and output, and we will consider some of these.

Input Peripherals

First of all, here are five types of equipment that provide variations to keyboard input.

Graphics Tablets. These devices (rectangular pads attached to the computer) allow you to draw pictures on the screen without having to press keys. The tablet represents the screen, and as you draw on it, the picture appears on the screen. The tablet usually has functions that allow you to change color, draw circles or rectangles, change the kind of line you are using, and so on. Some make it easy for you to trace pictures laid over the tablet. In this way students can create their own maps, diagrams, or other graphics on the screen.

Mice. A mouse is a device that you roll along the tabletop. It fits under your hand, with your fingers resting on a button. As you move it, an arrow on the screen moves in the direction of the mouse's motion. Options are presented in different areas of the screen. You slide the mouse to the option you want and click the button on the mouse to select it. Software that uses the mouse is designed so that you need to use the keyboard only when you want to input text, as in word processing.

Card Readers. These devices use punched cards for input, as the older computers did (Remember your old utility bills?). Now there are card readers made specifically for microcomputers. Many schools use them to enter information about students. Test results, for instance, can be marked on the card by filling in spaces with a pencil. The cards can then be collected and fed through the card reader, and the data stored permanently on disks. A computer program can analyze and report on the data. An advantage of this method is that only one computer is needed; data collection is done by hand at various sites and is usable by the computer.

Light Pens. A light pen is a device that looks like a pen and is used to input responses right on the screen. The user simply points the pen to an area of the screen and is able to answer questions, make moves in a game, draw lines, and so on. The computer reads the input through the pen; it "knows" what area of the screen the pen is pointing to. Thus, to choose an activity from a screen menu, you would just point to the activity desired and push a button on the pen, instead of having to type in your response.

Touch-sensitive Screens. Lately an even simpler way to use the screen for input has been developed. With a touch-sensitive screen, you don't even need a light pen. Simply pressing the screen with your finger will give the same result. These screens are often seen in airports or tourist spots. They let people get information by selecting what they want to know from menus.

Notice that all of these peripherals are alternatives to using the keyboard. The card reader, which is used mainly for large data-handling jobs, requires printed input. The other four are pressure-sensitive: Two of them use pressure on the screen, and the other two use pressure on a representation of the screen. These options not only make it easier or more convenient to perform some jobs, but for a range of people who have difficulty using the keyboard they may make it possible to use the computer.

All such peripherals must be connected to the computer in some way. With some computers, you put a card with memory chips into a slot inside the computer and attach a cable from the card to the device. With others, instead of opening the computer you attach a special cable to an outside connection. The principle is the same in all cases: You are enhancing the ability of the computer to read and interpret data.

Output Peripherals

In addition to the ordinary screen and printer output described in Chapter 1, a number of variations are available.

Screen Options.   Computer output is usually received on a screen. Recently, screen options have been multiplying. Standard computer monitors come in a wide range of price and quality, in color or monochrome. You can usually use your television set as a monitor. There are also many large-screen monitors on the market that allow you to display computer output to a large group. These last are relatively expensive (usually well over $1,000), and their quality can vary dramatically, but it is often necessary to have one for demonstration purposes in schools, and when they are widely used, the cost gets distributed.

Printer Options.   The second most common type of output device is a *printer.* Here again the options are numerous and growing. In printouts from cheaper dot-matrix printers, the dots that make up the characters are visible, making the text harder to read. Letter-quality printers use daisy wheels (wheels with all of the characters engraved on them) or similar devices, and are more expensive, but produce clearer printing. Special graphic printers let you print your computer drawings on paper. Some of these printers come with multicolor options.

Voice Synthesizers.   Voice synthesizers are growing in popularity. Computer experts have long been predicting that voice output will replace the need to read screen messages. This is possible, but the technology has been slow to develop. At present there are many voice synthesizers available for a variety of microcomputers. The speech sounds mechanical, and sometimes words are impossible to recognize, but this does not necessarily bother children. For young children, especially, voice output would seem to be a necessary ingredient for successful computer use.

Besides these input and output devices, there are peripherals for a wide range of other computer tasks, from increasing the computer's storage capacity to controlling robots. Here we will single out for special discussion two devices that can be interfaced with computers: *videodisks*, which can give your computer access to a wealth of visual information, and *modems*, which allow your computer to communicate with other computers around the world through your telephone.

Videodisks

How Videodisks Work

The input and output peripherals that we have just discussed are all integral to the operation of the computer; they are part of the computer system and modify or enhance it in some way. Videodisk players, on the other hand, are usually thought of as independent devices. You can purchase one, buy a disk for it, take it home, and play it without ever thinking of a computer. At the same time, though, videodisks are programmable; when they are interfaced with a computer, you can do anything that the computer could do alone, plus have access to anything on the disk.

What is a videodisk, and what can you do with it? Videodisks are recordings of thousands of optical frames: Many two-sided disks have over 100,000 frames. These can be single frames (snapshots) or frames that make up motion picture clips. With motion clips, you can also have audio accompaniment. The producer of the videodisk arranges the frames on the disk in any way he or she desires and provides you with a guide: With so many frames you could easily get lost. You can then look at still pictures, movie clips, or any frame from a movie clip.

Videodisks are similar in some ways to the floppy disks that you put into your computer's disk drive. Both store a large amount of information, any section of which can be accessed in a matter of seconds. Floppy disks store information encoded in numbers, and the computer has to interpret it, whereas videodisks encode optical information (pictures). Videocassettes also store video information, but this information is not easily accessible: You need to wind the tape to get to the spot where the picture is located. Disk technology is much faster than tape technology. You can use cassette audiotapes instead of floppy disks with your computer, but the same principle applies: Tapes must be wound to the right spot, relatively slowly, whereas disk information can be accessed almost instantly.

Videodisks thus provide a powerful medium for accessing visual material. The videodisk player comes with a set of functions that you control by means of buttons. Among these functions are the ability to

> Choose a frame number and move instantly to it
> Move step by step through the frames
> Move backward or forward through the disk
> Turn on or off either of the audio speakers
> Scan quickly through the frames in either direction

There is one important limitation to current videodisks. Unlike computer floppy disks, you cannot make your own videodisk; this must be done in a production center and costs a lot of money. Thus you buy what someone else has decided is worth producing. If this changes in the near future, as many people predict, videodisks could become much more popular than they are now. Videocassette recorders are cheaper than videodisk players, and they are more popular, even without instant access.

Applications

If instant access is the key to the videodisk, how can this be used in practice? Here are three possible ways:

> Imagine a shopping catalog recorded on a videodisk. Instead of looking at still photographs of the goods you want, you could, by typing in the frame or chapter number, instantly get an animated look at them in use.
> Putting together or repairing equipment is a job that is often difficult, in spite of illustrated manuals. With a videodisk you could watch the same step over and over, in slow or real-time motion.
> As a reference source, you could buy a disk containing film footage and still photographs of space-shuttle missions. You could flip to different views of the earth from space or examine, frame by frame, how the astronauts move in space.

The largest market for videodisks so far is for training people to do particular tasks. The army uses videodisks to train soldiers in weapons handling. Industry uses disks to train workers in equipment operation and assembly. Trainers find this medium an effective alternative to manuals or personal demonstration. So far, education has seen limited use of videodisks, although predictions for the future vary widely. Some people claim that in a few years every school will have them; others believe their use will decline.

How might videodisks be widely used in schools? One obvious answer is that they could assist in giving the kinds of training that schools provide —for example, in vocational training or science education. Another use is as a reference source: The availability of hundreds of thousands of frames worth of visual information per disk, ranging from movie clips to collections of original documents, means that teachers could have access to visual material in subjects that previously they could only try to describe—subjects such as world geography, for example, or scenes from space-shuttle missions.

A third possible use involves the interface of the videodisk with the computer. We mentioned this possibility earlier, but until now we have talked about the videodisk used by itself. Cable connections are now being sold to link microcomputers with videodisks, and in many cases authoring languages are provided that make it fairly easy to write a program that controls the videodisk player.

This development could be significant for educational use. Think about the software described in Chapter 2—the kind that uses maps, refers to people or places—in general, that uses anything that can be pictured. Then think of the value of having an actual screen image of such things, in either animated or still form, at your command. The computer can use the videodisk in a piece of software in any way in which the videodisk can be used by itself.

Imagine, for example, a videodisk lesson on world geography. Instead of using text alone to describe, or crude computer graphics to illustrate, various climatic regions or geographic features, this program uses movies, drawings, and photographs on videodisk to fly over, or zoom in on, deserts, river valleys, archipelagoes, and mountains. It also lets the student select parts of the globe to visit. Or, for example, a program on World War II could show the locations of famous battles, the people involved in them, and ground and aerial views of the battle sites, using photographs, film re-creations, and old film footage. In both of these programs the computer could show only computer text on the screen, or just pictures, or a combination of the two. Options could let the student slow down the action or speed it up.

There is obviously potential in all this for useful classroom application, but how much application we will actually see in schools is impossible to predict. An assortment of technological problems has, until now, hindered videodisk use. We have mentioned the inability of the user to record his or her own disk, so that schools can use only what someone else has produced. Also, there are two alternative kinds of videodisk systems, one using a laser to read the information on the disk and the other using a stylus electrode that moves across the disk. The ability to access individual frames that we have been describing is available only with the first, optical system.

These problems, plus the costs associated with these systems, have helped keep sales down. On the other hand, technological problems are often overcome, and acceptance of new technologies in education often takes some time. The day when every school will have its own videodisk system may actually dawn.

Modems

How Modems Work

Modems are devices that enable computers to communicate with other computers over telephone lines. The word *modem* is a combination of the beginning letters of the terms *modulate* and *demodulate*. *Modulate* refers to changing the kind of signal produced: Computers operate with digital signals, but telephone lines use acoustical signals. The modem changes the digital signal to an acoustical signal, so that information can pass from the computer through the telephone line, and then it changes the acoustical signal back to a digital signal (demodulates it), so that the computer on the other end can read it.

Modems come in many forms and prices, but they all involve connecting a computer to a telephone line. Some modems use actual telephones and two telephone jacks (one for the phone and one for the modem). Most modems for microcomputers (*micromodems*) have the telephone switching equipment built right into the modem. You attach the modem to the computer as you do other peripherals, connect the modem at the other end to a telephone jack, and use the software that comes with the modem. This software gives you various options: dialing an off-site computer, hanging up, and sending or receiving files.

Applications

The main uses for your modem were discussed in the section on off-site data bases in Chapter 2. To dial data-base services such as The Source or CompuServe from your microcomputer or your terminal, you need a modem. When you connect with the service, the software on the service's computer instructs you in how to use it. All such data bases are stored as computer files; when you are using them, you are communicating with a computer.

In addition, computer owners belong to computer networks. This is another way of communicating with an off-site computer via a modem. People can send and receive mail all around the country (or even the world) by subscribing to such a network and paying some fees, usually charged by the amount of time you use. Sometimes "billboard" services let you advertise to everyone on the network and read everyone else's notices.

Another form of special-purpose network is the mail service, which typically allows you to send mail to anyone in its range of services. If that person is a subscriber to the same network, the message is delivered on his or her computer. If not, the message is printed out and delivered by a conventional mail service.

Still another use of the modem involves interfacing two microcomputers, each equipped with the same kind of micromodem. If both machines are on at the same time and running the micromodem software, the two operators—who can be in the same room or across the continent —can send files back and forth. A "file" is something that you have created and saved on a disk—for example, a message that you have prepared using a word processor. The micromodem software can transfer your file from your disk drive, through your computer, over the telephone lines, and into the receiver's computer and onto his or her computer's disk drive.

A final example is the ability to "download" (or transfer) software from a large computer to a microcomputer. This type of service resembles a large data-base system, except that in this case what is being sent is not data but a program that your microcomputer can run. Educational software and games are prime candidates for downloading, so that both the home and the school are likely subscribers. Already in use, to a very limited degree, this type of service may become common. It would mean that instead of having to buy every piece of software that you wanted you could, in effect, rent it.

These examples illustrate the variety of communications jobs that a microcomputer can do. In effect, it can communicate with any other computer—microcomputer or mainframe—that is equipped for communication. As in other technological applications that we have discussed, there are limitations: You need the right kind of equipment to be compatible with the other party's computer. Since most microcomputers are incompatible with each other, how can the same software be downloaded to different machines? Whether or not we will see a great extension of microcomputer applications in the classroom will depend on many factors, among them this problem of computer compatibility; cost; and the degree of need for these applications that is felt by educators.

☐   THE COMPUTER AND OTHER MEDIA: NEW MODES OF COMMUNICATION   ☐

An important technological trend has been the linking of formerly separate media together. We have just seen how telephone systems can be part of computer systems. Conceivably, any signal that can be sent and received can become part of some applications system. A proliferation of means of transmitting signals — broadcast systems, microwave carriers, cable, optical fibers, communication satellites — has increased the power of transmissions and their capacity. This means that more people can communicate at once, and over longer distances. Messages can be sent in an increasing variety of ways.

From the user's point of view, one implication of all of this is an increase in communication possibilities. As we have seen in connection with electronic data-base and mail systems, people sitting at home in front of their microcomputers or computer terminals can communicate with other computers or with other people, via computers. Now let's consider two other applications that use the television set to provide interactivity.

Cable Television

Cable television has been with us for many years. Some time ago, the federal government mandated that certain cable television channels be set aside for educational or local use. Several communities have experimented with making cable television interactive, with the help of computers at the station and some kind of keypad attached to the computer at home for input. The viewer can communicate with the station by pressing a key; the computer reads and interprets the input. Some stations have conducted courses at home; the computer reads signals from the viewers who sign up, so that participants can answer questions or take exams. This kind of course is valuable for people who cannot leave their homes.

Another example of interactive cable use has allowed viewers to make instant decisions about programming — deciding, for instance, by pushing the appropriate key, whether the station should show the rest of the current program. Similarly, votes and referendums can be taken instantly, at home. Some people predict that in the future all elections will be handled this way, saving much time and paperwork in tabulating the votes.

Videotex Systems

These systems can also make your television set a more interactive medium. Screensful of information, combining graphics and text, are prepared by the videotex supplier, and these serve as a data base that you can access by means of a keypad attached to the television set. The information covered can be on any subject: news, weather, information about events or restaurants in the local area, and so on. In videotex, the data base consists of fully designed screensful, which can be rapidly accessed.

To select from the large data base, the user would choose the kind of information wanted from a menu and press the appropriate number on the keypad. Further selection might be necessary to pin down the exact screen display wanted. The computer managing the videotex system can then select and transfer the desired screen display to your television in a matter of seconds.

This kind of system has been in use in England, France, and Canada for a number of years, largely because these countries have centralized telecommunications ministries that set standards and help decide what applications to encourage. The United States relies on a free enterprise system, which to date has not perceived a demand for videotex in this country. In fact, tests by a number of companies have not found much need for it. Sometimes, however, the perception of need grows over a period of time, and there is still much interest in the United States in getting into the videotex field.

Part of the enthusiasm for videotex lies in the kind of interactivity it can promote. Receiving nicely designed screenfuls of information is only part of what you can do with it; the other part involves giving your input to the system. In other words, not only can you get information, but you could conceivably bank, shop, and make reservations with the system, provided these businesses were also linked to the system.

Several trends emerge from the variety of applications that we have covered in this chapter, trends that are likely to influence the shape of new technologies in the future and the way we use them.

1. New methods of input and output have been implemented. What some people call the "sensory system" of the computer no longer means just typing and reading. A variety of methods involving touch can provide input, and many researchers are hard at work on improving voice input. Voice output is fairly widely used and will probably improve in quality.
2. Storage and retrieval capacities are constantly being increased. This means that larger data bases are available, more complex programs are possible, and graphic output has become more complex.
3. Electronic connections among various types of media are increasing. Media hitherto thought of as separate are now part of one

system. Television, telephones, computers, and broadcast systems can be combined for various applications.

4. These three trends are all factors in increasing the interactivity between the user and other computers, or among people using computers. A proliferation of networks and data bases has resulted in new media for communication.

☐   AN ELECTRONICALLY CONNECTED SOCIETY?   ☐

Our examples have been taken from existing applications, but we can use the trends that emerge from them to point to a future in which people may increasingly interact through computer-driven technology to conduct their daily business. This is not to say that society will elect to go in this direction; we cannot know all the factors that determine the future. Many analysts and futurologists, however, have extrapolated from present trends and come up with scenarios of what the future might hold in store for us. Let's describe a little of this realm of the possible here, so that in the next chapter we can discuss the implications and issues that derive from our technologies.

Imagine, then, a world in which almost every operation that uses information that can be stored in computer files is handled by computers. Here are some possibilities:

A doctor trying to help a person who has been taken ill at an airport while traveling could have access to the patient's medical records, held in a data base in the patient's own hospital, and could thus be able to diagnose the problem on the spot.

Access to buildings or offices could be controlled by voice input or fingerprint input instead of by keys. The building's central computer would store files containing the information it needs to recognize these.

Imagine the "cashless" society, to which we are apparently already on the way. All transactions, from shopping in stores to paying bills, would be handled by subtracting directly from the buyer's account and adding to the payee's account, handled, of course, by a centralized computer. We would no longer need cash but would carry around one card, like present-day credit cards.

Imagine newspapers printed out directly on your home printer instead of being mass-produced and distributed. They could be personalized to print only a selection of the news you want, by area or by type of topic.

Books could also be made available through your home computer; you could have one that you wanted printed out on your printer, and you would be charged accordingly.

Finally, practically all transactions that you need to make could be done from your home: ordering anything, communicating with anyone.

You could probably go on filling out this hypothetical sketch (and this might be a good activity for students to do when talking about our technologically oriented society). The point is that in all of these examples, the use, transaction, and communication of data could be handled electronically. This obviously has implications for the way our society lives and works, and we turn now to a consideration of these implications.

□4□
Issues: Technology and Society

This book has so far examined a variety of techniques that can help us get across to students many of the important concepts and skills of the social studies. But as we computerize our classrooms, this same technology is causing changes in the world outside. It is giving rise to new social issues; some say that computers are shifting us from the industrial age to the information age, that we are in the midst of a social and cultural revolution brought on by the rapid diffusion of new technology.

If this is all true, then it certainly is something we should teach about. We should teach about how the standards of privacy and of search and seizure have changed with the advent of electronic surveillance and computer data banks; we cannot ignore in our economics courses the rapid rise of high-tech industry or the inflationary effects of electronic fund transfer. As teachers of citizenship, we must prepare our students to live and participate in a world where "information is power" and where the understanding and control of technology is a primary political factor.

In this chapter we discuss four general issues of technology and society: equity, privacy, computers in the workplace, and the politics of information. Each of these issues should find a place in your school's social studies curriculum. For each issue we present scenarios, a discussion of several points of view on it, and some ideas on how to teach about it.

It is interesting that there is not yet any instructional software to help us teach these issues; perhaps that's best. Using such software might be like letting the fox babysit the chickens.

□   EQUITY   □

Unequal Access to Computers

• In a recent survey in California, boys and girls in the fourth through twelfth grades were asked to describe how they would use computers when they were 30 years old. Boys said they would use computers for financial analysis, data processing, and games. Girls thought they would use them for housework. One sixth-grade girl wrote: "When I am 30, I'll have a computer that has long arms and that can clean the house and cook meals, and another computer to pay for groceries and stuff" ("Equal Time for Women," *Discover*, January 1984, p. 25).

• The Suburban Parents Association held bake sales, car washes, and a carnival to raise money to increase the ratio of computers to students in the district from 1 computer for every 8 students to the better ratio of 1 computer for every 4 students. In the nearby city, however, the school district proudly announced that it was going to install 1 computer in each of the 16 elementary schools in the inner city in September.

• Sam begged his parents to give him a computer for his eighth birthday, since all of his friends had gotten one when they turned eight. When his grandparents presented it to him, his mother asked Sam to let his grandfather, who was visiting from out of town, help him set it up. Sam whispered that he would rather wait for his father to come home, since "old people don't know anything about computers."

We are living in the computer age. But it seems that some of us have greater access to computers and their benefits than others. This trend is also likely to continue in the future. Surveys have shown that computers are mainly used by males, the young (under 40), and the economically secure. Among the young there is also the impression (fostered by advertising campaigns and television) that computers are the domain of the young, and that older people just cannot understand these "newfangled contraptions."

So the issue of computer equity—that is, equal access to computers and technology and to the benefits that access to them brings—becomes one that must be added to any study in the social studies classroom of overall equity in our own society and in the world. Computer literacy—defined as whatever a person needs to know about and be able to do with computers in order to function competently in our society—is fast becoming a basic survival skill. Some groups of people, though, are finding that skill difficult to acquire, for a variety of reasons.

Women and Computers

There has long been the notion in the minds of many men and women throughout the world that women and mathematics are incompatible. Because of this, many women have suffered from "math anxiety," or a seeming inability to grasp mathematical concepts, during and after their school years. Since computers are commonly viewed as "number crunchers," this math anxiety may carry over to computers. The fact that some people believe that computers are too complex to be understood by the average woman has fostered an attitude that has kept some women out of the computer and information-science fields.

The gap between men and women and their experiences with computers starts in elementary school and grows through high school. A study by the California Department of Education revealed that only 37 percent of the students enrolled in high school computer courses in 1980 were girls. A nationwide poll of 17-year-olds has shown that nearly twice as many boys as girls take computer programming classes ("Equal Time for Women," p. 152).

The situation does not change much after high school. The more advanced the computer training, the fewer women enroll. At MIT, for instance, the male graduate students in computer science outnumber the females nearly 10 to 1.

The inequity of this differential in computer use by the sexes is a problem that has only recently been recognized and studied by educators and psychologists. The problem does not seem to be that women are incapable of learning about computers. On the contrary, some of the very traits many women are endowed with and that are considered by some to be feminine, such as patience and attention to detail, are particularly desirable in computer specialists.

Instead, the barrier seems to be a social one. At a very early age, many women are encouraged to believe that computers are not for them. For example, few girls venture into video arcades where many young people get their first exposure to computers. Much of the war- or destruction-oriented software developed for the machines used there is designed by men and appeals primarily to boys.

At some schools, teachers report that boys fight to get to use the computer, while the girls sit back. Computer classes are filled to capacity, so there is no motivation to go out and recruit those who are a bit timid about getting started on the computer. Computer "hackers" who are often male, and sometimes antisocial, can also be obstacles to girls' getting to use the computers in schools where computer facilities are limited or loosely monitored.

As awareness of this problem increases, there is real hope that the situation can be changed quickly. Since computing is a new field, there is a chance that women can be encouraged to become comfortable with computers before expectations and stereotypes become set. Several organizations, such as the American Women in Science and the American

Association of University Women, are conducting workshops and sending women into schools to talk to students about the rewards of technical careers. There is also an organization called the Association for Women in Computing that is aiding women who are already committed to careers in computing. Computer courses for the less mathematically inclined are also being offered at more schools and universities. Many people who take these classes go on to try more sophisticated computer classes. Software to help housewives manage their budgets is also becoming available.

New software, written to appeal to girls in the middle grades, is also being marketed. Programs such as JENNY OF THE PRAIRIE and THE HOUSE THAT JILL BUILT are now available. JENNY OF THE PRAIRIE features a plucky heroine who must survive on her own after being separated from her wagon train in the 1840s. THE HOUSE THAT JILL BUILT allows the user to build a dream house, while learning about styles of architecture along the way.

One of the most encouraging factors is the existence of job opportunities in the computer field that are multiplying faster than people can take advantage of them. As the market continues to expand, few people will care whether the many available jobs are filled by men or by women as long as they have the right qualifications. Our schools must be encouraged to provide a chance for both girls and boys to acquire those qualifications. Talking about the problem in social studies classes as part of the larger issue of sexual discrimination can also help. The subject of women and computers might also make an interesting case study for the issues of unequal opportunity or the persistence of stereotypes.

Socioeconomic Differences in Computer Use

Women are only part of a larger group that is being denied, for a variety of reasons, access to computer training. Despite the fact that the price of a personal computer has fallen dramatically in the last few years, there is still a large segment of the population for whom a computer remains a low-priority, luxury item. This holds true for some school districts also. For these schools, teachers have to come first.

There is a certain danger in letting this situation remain at status quo. As technology accelerates, the people who are left behind or who are slow to join in the computer revolution will have a harder and harder time catching up with those who have some computer literacy. People who are familiar with computers are likely to be the ones to get the better jobs now and in the future. People who are afraid of computers and technology—and many people (such as women or older people) are, or are thought to be — will be relegated to do the poorly paid menial tasks that will shut them out even more definitively.

There is a time-tested solution to this problem: education. Through the schools, young people can become accustomed to today's technology and in doing so prepare for tomorrow's technology. Training programs also have to be devised for retraining older people to use the latest and best of the currently available technology.

Unfortunately, though, as in the case of women and computers, the opportunity to grow and keep up with new developments in computer use is not being equally offered by the schools. As we said to start with, cost is a large factor in this. But people who already have had some contact with computers, such as the parents in our scenario of the Suburban Parents Association, recognize the need for computers in the schools and have taken the matter into their own hands. Across the country, their efforts to get computers into their childrens' schools is being duplicated over and over again.

This effort is not being replicated by many poorer rural and inner-city districts, because parents and schools there do not recognize the need for computers as well and also have difficulty affording them. Some help may be on the way in the form of federal funds or grants from corporations that will enable schools to get computers. Once the computers are in the schools, teachers and administrators must be educated on the best way to make use of them. Being able to brag that a school has a computer is no help to the students if the computer is kept in the administrative offices or if it is used only to run preprogrammed software. A survey of many inner-city schools revealed that this was how their computers were being used. Although running preprogrammed software will help students to become familiar with the computer, it is also important that they learn how the computer works by learning to program.

Worldwide Computer Use

The problems of inequity in access to computers in this country is only a small model for a larger global problem. Computers have already widened the gap between the developed and the underdeveloped nations of the world, and will continue to do so. As computers make research and development easier and the production of goods — from breeding livestock to building rockets — faster and better, it is going to be more difficult for underdeveloped nations to compete. Technology costs money, and sometimes it is years before those costs are recovered. Many nations do not have the funds or the technical expertise that are needed if they are to catch up.

Some Lesson Suggestions

These problems, of course, are all extensions of issues that are already part of the social studies curriculum. They are an added dimension, though, that we all must be reminded exists. To do that with students, you might try some of the following:

- Have students make a survey of the computers in your school or school district. Have them count the number of computers and report on how they are used: for administration, or instruction, or both. Also have them determine what groups are using the computer: what content areas, how many females, how many males, age groups, and so forth, and how much time these groups are spending at the machine. All of this information can be graphed or charted by students by hand or on the computer (see the section on graphing programs in Chapter 2). Discuss the conclusions of the survey with students. Does it seem that more computer time is going to administration or instruction? Who is using the computer? Tell students that national surveys have shown that more males than females are using computers. Are the statistics that students have collected consistent with these trends? Ask students how they think more women could be encouraged to use computers. A copy of the students' final report could be forwarded to the principal or superintendent, along with their recommendations on how to get more computers into the hands of more students.
- Do a study with students of the kinds of advertisements for computer hardware and software that appear in magazines or on television. Who are these advertisements aimed at? Who appears in the commercials? What are their relationships? What are some of the messages they give? (One favorite message is that if you really love your child you will give him or her a computer.) How do students think parents respond to these advertisements? What message is being given about the connection between computers and future financial success, or between computers and older people?
- Despite the fact that computer prices have fallen dramatically, a personal home computer is still out of the reach of many families. Have students research the prices of the various popular computers on the market, including the cost of monitors, printers, disk drives, and other equipment. Then have them try to fit one of these systems into the budget of a family of four with an income of between $15,000 and $25,000. What are their conclusions? To make their study more interesting, talk about all of the things that the com-

puter may be used for in the home in the future. In what ways are
people who cannot afford the latest technology going to be left out?
For example, what will happen if national voting is done via personal home computer?

• The typist stepped away from the computer console for just a
moment. While he was gone, the wind blew some records off his
desk, mixing the credit information sheets of Ben Stone with those
of another client. When the typist returned and began typing what
he thought was Stone's file into the computer, Stone's credit rating
was entered as poor rather than excellent. This information was
passed on to bank, credit, and insurance companies' computers
everywhere with the touch of a key. Stone's request for a credit card
was turned down, and he got a call from his insurance company
demanding that he pay the entire yearly premium for his car insurance at once. It took him weeks to straighten out the confusion in
his records.

• Using a software program called LOCKSMITH, John was able to
illegally unlock the codes that supposedly protected all of the computer games available at the local library from being copied. He
made four copies of each game: one to keep, and three to sell to his
friends. The original games cost $29 apiece. John sold his copies for
$10 apiece: since he had paid $2 for each disk, he made an $8 profit
on each, or a total of $24.

• A terrorist group sent a film purporting to show President Reagan in a secret meeting with Palestine Liberation Organization (PLO)
leaders to the three major television networks. In the film, Reagan
was seen and heard to give a pledge to "bring Israel to its knees" in
return for PLO help in invading Iran. Film experts were called in,
but they were unable to determine whether the film was real or
whether it had been computer-generated. The three networks decided to show it anyway, with a brief introductory caveat.

As the era of technology continues, public concern over the invasion
of individual privacy by computers and other machines in the control of
unscrupulous or careless people grows. Today, computer data banks con-

tain a great deal of information about most average Americans. Our banking, credit, and insurance records, and even our medical records are part of some computer's memory. Government computers also have on file our tax records, census information, and the facts that we indicated when we applied for our driver's licenses and other documents.

We all hope to exert some control over this mass of information that has been collected about us. We are concerned about how that information will be disseminated and for what purpose. The safety and protection of that information also comes into question every time we hear about the success of another computer pirate or about a new computer mixup.

Technology and the Law

Congress addressed the privacy issue in the Omnibus Crime Control Act and in the Privacy Act, passed in 1974. The former deals with electronic surveillance and sets forth the circumstances in which one can legally gain private information about an individual or group by techniques such as wiretapping. Its principles and provisions may be extended to cover the interception of data and messages sent from computer terminals over public telephone lines.

The Privacy Act of 1974 addresses the rights of individuals with regard to the personal data collected about them that is contained in federal data banks. Its principles and provisions can also be extended to include privately owned pools of data about individuals, since the potential dangers are nearly identical.

Under the Privacy Act, individuals do have the right to know what personal information is in a data bank and to correct any inaccuracies. (How to find out about those inaccuracies quickly may be another question.) The type of information that a data handler can collect about an individual and the way in which that information can be combined with information about him or her from other data bases is also restricted. The law also established a Privacy Protection Study Commission to report on the Act's implementation and on other privacy areas that need to be addressed. Areas in which the commission has noted that more protection and new regulations or guidelines are needed include the protection of privacy during routine information gathering by the government and other private and public organizations (such as credit agencies, hospitals, and schools) and during the informal collection and sharing of information among organizations. Currently there is little legal protection for the transfer of personal data that is not explicitly recognized as confidential information.

Intrusive Technology

Both of these Acts are very difficult to enforce, though, and rapid technological development only worsens the problem. Our privacy is going to become harder and harder to protect in the years to come as technology makes it easier for information to enter and leave our homes through our computers, our television sets, and other electronic devices. For example, an interactive cable system (one connected to a television set and a cable network) can scan a connected household to record such information as whether a television set is turned on or off, what channel is being viewed, and the last response button pushed. Other home technology systems use the same technique to detect fire, smoke, sound, and even movement (yours or an intruder's) within a house. (A positive side of these systems, though, is that besides just sending in an alarm, the system is connected to a central computer that can also send information on the architecture of the house, the presence of hazardous materials, and the occupants' medical history to the fire department.)

Utility companies are using similar systems to monitor energy loads. This might become intrusive if the utility decides to act against those customers who are not cooperating with energy conservation programs.

The interception of information through unauthorized tapping into data banks is also a growing problem. Patient, technologically skilled pirates have been able to enter the memories of computers in banks, insurance companies, police departments, schools, and even the Defense Department. With a few keystrokes they have been able to move money from one account to another, pay unauthorized insurance claims, wipe out criminal records, and change grades. In the plot of the movie *War Games*, it was an intrusion of this kind that almost caused World War III.

Technological pirates have also been known to use the telephone company's long-distance lines for free and to make unauthorized copies of software, doing the authors out of their rightful royalties. This is, of course, why computer software is so expensive. Protecting the information on disks from being copied is almost impossible, so companies have to try to get their profits immediately, from the first copies sold of an original piece of software.

Industrial espionage has also become more cutthroat. Pirates break into companies' computers to steal plans or look at marketing information. Such a spying operation even occurred during a simulation game about fictitious start-up companies played by student teams at the Harvard Business School. The school has since introduced a course on business ethics.

The Computer and the Camera

Using the computer, it is now possible to make composites of photographs or to alter images in such a way that the changes may not be detectable. This means, for example, that a photograph could be put together supposedly showing John F. Kennedy greeting Fidel Castro years ago in Miami. Shadows would cross each man's face at consistent angles, their clothing would be of the right style for the times, and their faces would reflect their ages and conflicting concerns. The photograph would not reveal that the two men had never met and that the image had, in fact, been created by a computer.

This has some very disconcerting ramifications for historians, in particular. Realistic-looking photographs, now prized for their veracity, may be harder to trust in the future. As this technique of creating fabricated photographs is extended to film, the traditional acceptance of journalistic photographs and film as having been recorded from life may be difficult to sustain.

A further step may occur in the next decade or so, when techniques for simulating realistic-looking images of people are completely developed. "News" announcements about impending disasters or nuclear attacks might be delivered by a synthetic Dan Rather or Ronald Reagan. Terrorists, the CIA, and the KGB could make all kinds of claims, and back them up, with realistic-looking film or still photographs.

The one consolation is that most of this technology is not completely developed at this point and that computer-created images are extremely time-consuming to prepare. Because the images are mathematically created, they can take millions or more calculations for each picture. Of course, computers are helping to speed up some of that "number crunching," so that the images can be created in less time. Critics also point out, however, that it may be difficult to fool people whose perceptions are so attuned to recognizing their own kind.

All of this aside, the central issue remains the same. History may never be the same again if bogus photographs that cannot be distinguished by experts from the real thing begin to emerge. For a long time, people interested in the future have urged that we in the social studies need to interject projections of the future into our courses. Teaching students to question the validity of photographic evidence may be a place to start.

Some Lesson Suggestions

Privacy and ethics have certainly always been issues studied as part of the social studies, but again, current technology adds some new issues and ramifications to that study. Here are some lesson suggestions for starting to take a look at the issue:

- Have students make a list of all the kinds of information that is collected on them from the time they are born until they graduate from high school. After they have completed their list, have them put a *P* (for private) after all the items on the list that they believe should remain confidential and be prepared to give a reason why — even if that reason is just that they feel that it is no one else's business but their own. Discuss with them why privacy is such an emotional issue in this country. Ask them to put a *C* (for computerized) after all the items on their list that are likely to be recorded on computers? What are the dangers of having such information on computers? Ask them whether they know their rights to find out what is in their records and to correct inaccuracies, as they are stated in the Privacy Act of 1974.
- The temptation to copy commercially produced computer games from friends or to break the code and enter a forbidden computer's memory has been too much for many bright young computer enthusiasts. Unlocking a computer's secrets is often seen as a game, rather than as the illegal act that it is under the copyright law. Discuss the ramifications of computer piracy with your students. How would they feel if they had created an original book, artwork, invention, or piece of software, and it was copied illegally? What do students think should be done about computer pirates?
- For any period of history from the 1860s to the present that you are studying, ask students how our understanding of that period might be changed if a phony computer-created photograph (that experts certify as real) showed up. Ask them what the photograph would be of and how that might start speculation that a particular interpretation of history might be wrong. Discuss with them the possibility that photographs and film will no longer be proof that an event has occurred.

☐   TECHNOLOGY IN THE WORKPLACE   ☐

Here is a fictional example of how changes in computer technology might affect workers in industry today.

The Acme Stove Company is not a high-tech firm. For many years it has manufactured and repaired wood stoves for cooking and heating. It is family owned and has fewer than 50 employees. Yet technology has had a major effect on the nature of the workplace at Acme, and on the people who do the work there. Consider . . .

• Ann, a low-ranking typist who nevertheless gets special privileges and an extra week's vacation, because she is the only one who has figured out how to get reports from the firm's new computerized accounting system.

• Jim, the senior repairman in the shop, who was passed over for promotion because he has not yet learned to operate the computer-aided drill press used to make holes in the stoves.

• Molly, who was fired last week for refusing to spend more than five hours a day sitting in front of the word processor's cathode-ray tube. A union publication had suggested that the tubes can cause disease in some people.

• Henry, the young kid who knows nothing about the stove business but was promoted over more senior workers because of his ability to fix the new Computer Assisted Design machines in the shop.

• Kathleen, owner of the company, who cannot make a decision without consulting Henry and Ann, since they have sole control over the information she needs.

Other forms of technology have changed the Acme workplace in the past: the change from water to steam and then to electric power, for the machinery; the growth of national transportation networks that made theirs a national rather than a regional market; the new metals that allowed them to make much lighter yet much more efficient stoves. But none of these changes occurred as swiftly as the computerization of the company. The previous changes were thought about and planned over many years—decades, in most cases. The people undergoing the change understood the new machines, because they were not very different from what they had been using before. And they could see and touch the old technologies.

Computers were different. It took less than a year to consider and purchase the electronic accounting, ordering, and shipping system. The day it first arrived, no one understood how it worked or where all the information was being kept. The same was true for the Computer Assisted Design machines. They did not even resemble the old drill presses and lathes.

They had no dials, no gauges, nothing you could put a micrometer on—only a keyboard and a video screen with numbers on it. And the word processors were like magic toys: Your letters and invoices got printed in the next room somewhere, and the things made no noise when you typed. Even though just about all of the Acme employees were well trained, none of them had been trained to use these machines in their colleges or high schools. In most of their courses and textbooks, this new technology was hardly even mentioned.

The Issues

Computer technology has changed the physical aspects of the shop at Acme Stove Company, as well as the politics of the workplace. Some people and products have benefited from the change, and others have taken a back seat. Changes like this are taking place throughout the economy, and they are happening quickly. As our students prepare for life in the workplace, they need to be aware of the issues that these changes raise.

Training and Job Preparation.   There is no way that people today can prepare with confidence for the jobs of 20 years from now. No one at Acme was prepared to use computers in his or her work; the computerization of the workplace was not thought about back in the days when these workers were in college and trade school. And even if they had been trained to use the computers that existed while they were in training, it would not have done them any good: The machines used at Acme today are far, far different from the machines of 20 years ago.

This training issue certainly has ramifications for our social studies students as they contemplate their own futures and make career decisions. Few of them will engage in a single line of work all their lives; most of them will pursue two or three careers, as rapid technological change in the workplace alters the jobs that need to be done.

What they need, in order to be successful at a place like Acme today or at any work site in the future, is skill in figuring things out for themselves—as Ann and Henry did, in the example. Part of this skill comes in not being afraid of new technology; another part is in learning how to learn. Both of these skills are part of the traditional repertoire of the social studies.

Labor Health and Safety.   Just as the industrial revolution spawned movements to protect the health and safety of workers in the new and dangerous factory full of machines, so the coming of the computer to the workplace has given birth to modern-day concerns about the cathode-ray tube and the computer environment. Typists turned word processor operators will tell you that the new work is different: There is much less moving about, much more staring at the same spot, much more time spent just keying in information. Although the machine increases their efficiency, it also makes their work monotonous and one-sided. And who knows what the long-term effects are of staring at letters on a video screen? (Not enough data is in yet, but there has been some concern that certain kinds of video displays can cause blindness. Screens, however, are being improved all the time for easy-on-the-eye viewing.)

Decision Making. It used to be that business decisions were made without all the information that the decision maker needed. The advent of the information age, brought about largely by computer technology, has completely reversed this situation. Now the decision makers get too much data, data that they often do not understand or are not sure how to fit into the decisions they have to make. People like Henry and Ann, at the Acme Stove Company—who can turn data into useful information—will become more and more necessary to business. The ease with which computers can produce charts, graphs, and statistics (see the section on graphics and statistical packages, in Chapter 2) leads to a plethora of such items facing the decision maker. So the skill needed for the future is not so much in finding and creating information but in selecting what is relevant and in relating that data to the problem at hand. Again, these are classic social studies skills that are finding new application in the computer age.

Information as Economic Power. Success and power in the workplace in the United States has often been earned through efficient work habits and mechanical know-how. The new route to power, however, is in the management and control of information. The person who can access and make sense out of all the data that the company computer collects and stores will have the boss's ear more than will the competent mechanic. This shift of emphasis in the workplace can only lead to a change in general social values. There is no question that these kinds of issues are ripe for discussion and analysis in the social studies classroom.

Some Lesson Suggestions

It is not easy to teach about these issues. There is no textbook, and no tradition of lessons and methods. But here are some places to start.

- A case-study approach is probably best, using examples such as the Acme Stove Company that provide the students with concrete and personal examples of the problems and opportunities of computers

in the workplace. Students and their parents will certainly be able
to add to the Acme example with cases of their own.
- History is another fine source of cases that raise exactly these issues.
  The Luddites, in nineteenth-century England, make an interesting
  and remarkable parallel study. The change from cottage to factory
  systems of manufacture in nineteenth-century New England — with
  its accompanying revolution in workers' life-styles and in the roles
  of women — provides another good example of these issues.
- Finally, literature — from the novels of Charles Dickens, to Kurt
  Vonnegut's *Player Piano*, to Alvin Toffler's *The Third Wave* — can
  help us raise these issues with our students.

☐ ──────────────── INFORMATION AND POLITICAL POWER ──────────────── ☐

Advances in computer technology have important implications for participatory democracy. Here is a fictional example to illustrate some of
those implications.

- Vincent O'Malley was descended from a line of politicians. He
learned from dad and granddad how to serve the people and get the
vote out. Vinny had friends in high places and in low places. He
won his elections handily, but not without hard work pressing the
flesh and reminding people of who their friends were.

Harley O'Toole spent most of his growing-up years in the library.
He learned how to find information — from books, journals, indexes,
and, most recently, from computer printouts and data banks. No
illegal electronic break-ins: just knowledge of the methods for accessing public and unprotected information files. Harley put this skill to
work for him when he ran for the City Council against Vincent
O'Malley.

While Vinny was in the smoke-filled room making what he
thought were "deals," Harley and his staff were combining data files
from public records. By comparing the names of registered voters
(pulled from the city clerk's computer file) with the names of people
who owned homes assessed at more than $60,000 (from the tax
assessor's computer file), Harley developed a list of potentially afflu-
ent voters and sent out flyers appealing to them for funds. They
turned out to be heavy campaign contributors and to be more dissat-
isfied than the average voter with Vinny's populist image. This group
of supporters, along with personal (but computer-generated) letters

mailed to members of various fraternal organizations and community clubs, helped Mr. O'Toole win a narrow victory over the incumbent.

The clever use of information technology won the election for O'Toole. O'Malley had access to the same information, since it was all a matter of public record, but he did not make any use of it. This election, and other situations in which computer technology is the gatekeeper to valuable information, should raise in our students' minds important issues in democracy:

How Public Should the Government Be? Most of the data that O'Toole used to win his election was in the hands of the city government, or at least in the computer files of the government. Governments at all levels are by far the largest keepers of information. As a larger proportion of our government's records begins to be kept on floppy disks and magnetic tape, the nature of access to that information by citizens is altered. On the one hand, computer wizards like O'Toole find it easier to get, compile, and make use of the information they need. It would have taken O'Toole months to compile his lists by hand from paper records. On the other hand, O'Malley finds it difficult to look up papers in the clerk's office casually, as he used to. The data is no longer in file cabinets, only in computer storage. Technology has changed the way we get information, making the government more public for some, yet less public for others.

Overdependence on Technology in Governing. One of the scenarios in Chapter 1 described an "electronic town meeting" at which citizens, in a very direct form of democracy, voted via computer on the issues of the day. Rather than depend on elected representatives to help them govern, they were now relying on electronic devices. Can this dependence on machinery — machinery that can allow an unprecedented directness to our democracy — have any negative aspects? Like candidate O'Toole, the voters in the electronic meeting never met their fellow citizens at the meeting for a face-to-face discussion, calling instead on their private sources of information and their keyboard connection to the world. In a sense, their brand of direct democracy is wonderfully accountable to the people, since the people get to vote on every issue. In another sense, the private nature of the process and the lack of public discourse and face-to-face discussion of issues may take us further from a responsive and accountable government.

Some Lesson Suggestions

These are certainly appropriate issues for the social studies classroom. Here are some good ways to teach them.

- Have students write scenarios of possible future developments in voting and elections—both good and bad—that might be made possible through technology. These scenarios can form the basis for class discussion.
- Another way to reflect on the power of information is to let a group of students play a card game, but allow one of the students to have access to information on what cards the other players hold. See who wins the game; then relate this outcome to O'Toole's election and to the power of information in general.
- Finally, have students find out how the local city or town government keeps its information on voting registration, property tax appraisals, and other matters. Is it accessible only by computer? How can citizens get to see it?

☐ _____ CONCLUSION _____ ☐

In this chapter we have only had time to look at a few of the issues raised by the increasing role of technology in our society. Although it is impossible to cover all of the issues, either here or in the classroom, we need to be aware of them, since the social studies classroom may be the only place in a student's school career where they are discussed. Also, as we have mentioned, such issues make a great place to start your consideration of computers, especially if an adequate supply of hardware and software is not yet available to your classes.

Ideally, computers are already available to you (or soon will be), and we hope that the material in this book has provided a useful introduction on how to start using them in your classroom. In addition, we believe we have given you a bit of vision about the future of the computer and the social studies, as well as some insight into other technologies that will give you and your students more exciting tools to use in your joint study of the social studies.

GUIDE TO RESOURCES

INDEX

APPENDIX

Guide to Resources

	SECTION ONE: PRINTED MATERIALS	

General Resources

Books

Ahl, David H., ed. *Computers in Science and Social Studies: A Sourcebook of Ideas.* Morristown, NJ: Creative Computing Press, 1983.

Colburn, Peter. *Practical Guide to Computers and Education.* Reading, MA: Addison-Wesley, 1982.

Diem, Richard A. *Computers in the Social Studies Classroom,* NCSS "How to Do It" Series 2, No. 14. Washington, DC: National Council for the Social Studies, 1981.

Educational Software Directory: A Subject Guide to Microcomputer Software. Littleton, CO: Libraries Unlimited, 1982.

EPIE Institute. *TESS: The Educational Software Selector.* Water Mill, NY: EPIE Institute, 1985.

Forrester, Jay W. *Urban Dynamics.* Cambridge, MA: MIT Press, 1969.

Glenn, Allen, and Don Rawitsch. *Computing in the Social Studies Classroom.* Eugene, OR: International Council for Computers in Education, University of Oregon, 1984.

Hodges, James O. *A Bibliography of Microcomputer Software for Social Studies Educators, 1982.* Virginia Department of Education, P.O. Box 6-Q, Richmond, VA 23216.

International Software Directory. Volume 2, *Microcomputers.* Fort Collins, CO: Imprint Software, Ltd., 1982. (Also available as International Software Database through DIALOG.)

Lengel, James G. *Computer Considerations for Vermont Schools, 1984.* Vermont State Department of Education, Montpelier, VT 05602.

Meadows, Donella H., Dennis L. Meadows, Jorgem Randers, and William W. Behrens III. *The Limits to Growth.* New York: Universe Books, 1973.

Swift's Educational Software Directory, 1984. Sterling Swift, Austin, TX 78704.

Taylor, Robert P. *The Computer in the School: Tutor, Tool, Tutee.* New York: Teachers College Press, 1980.

"Technology and the Social Studies," *Social Education* (National Council for the Social Studies) 47 (May 1983): entire issue.

Periodicals

Classroom Computer Learning. Peter Li, Inc., 2451 East River Rd., Dayton, OH 45439.

Creative Computing. 39 East Hanover Ave., Morristown, NJ 07950.

Electronic Learning. Scholastic, Inc., 730 Broadway, New York, NY 10003.

Journal of Educational Technology Systems. Baywood Publishing Co., Inc., 120 Marine St., Farmingdale, NY 11735.

Media and Methods. American Society of Educators, 1511 Walnut St., Philadelphia, PA 19102.

Personal Computing. Hayden Publishing Co., Inc., P.O. Box 2942, Boulder, CO 80322.

Social Education. National Council for the Social Studies, 3501 Newark St., NW, Washington, DC 20016.

T.H.E. Journal (Technical Horizons in Education). Information Synergy, Inc., 2922 S. Daimler St., Santa Ana, CA 92705.

The Computing Teacher. International Council for Computers in Education, University of Oregon, 1787 Agate St., Eugene, OR 97493.

The Social Studies. Heldref Publications, 4000 Albemarle St., NW, Washington, DC 20016.

Other General Resources

MicroSIFT (Microcomputer Software and Information for Teachers). Northwest Regional Educational Laboratory, 300 SW 6th Ave., Portland, OR 97204. (Software evaluations and occasional articles and releases.)

NCSS Courseware Evaluation Guidelines, 1984. National Council for the Social Studies, 3501 Newark St., NW, Washington, DC 20016.

Special Interest Group: Computers and Social Education (SIG-CASE). c/o Charles S. White, Education 325-OIC, Indiana University, Bloomington, IN 47405. (Organization of social studies teachers.)

Classroom Applications

Simulation

Noonan, Larry. "Computer Simulations in the Classroom," *Creative Computing* 7 (October 1981): 132–138.

Roberts, Nancy. *An Introduction to Computer Simulations: The System Dynamics Approach.* Reading, MA: Addison-Wesley, 1983.

Data Bases and Networking

Cook, William J. *The Joy of Computer Communication.* New York: Dell Publishing Co., 1984.

Directory of On-line Data Bases. Cuadra Associates, 2001 Wilshire Blvd., Santa Monica, CA 90403.

Grossbrenner, Alfred. *Personal Computer Communications.* New York: St. Martin's Press, 1983.

Hunter, Beverly. "Problem Solving with Data Bases," *The Computing Teacher* 12 (May 1985): 20–27.

Neumann, Robert. "Data Banks: Opening the Door to a World of Information," *Electronic Learning* 2 (November/December 1982): 56–60.

Traberman, Tama. "Using Microcomputers to Teach Global Studies," *Social Education* 48 (February 1984): 130–137.

Using Data Bases in Social Studies. Social Science Education Consortium, 855 Broadway, Boulder, CO 80302.

Word Processing

Daiute, Colette. *Writing and Computers.* Reading, MA: Addison-Wesley, 1983.

Fluegelman, Andrew, and Jeremy Hewes. *Writing in the Computer Age.* New York: Doubleday, Quantum Press, 1983.

Fisher, Glenn. "Word Processing: Will It Make All Kids Love to Write?" *Instructor* 92 (February 1983): 87–88.

Computer-related Technologies

Campbell, Jeremy. *Grammatical Man.* New York: Simon & Schuster, 1982.

Howitt, Doran. "Computer Aided Design for All," *Infoworld*, December 3, 1984, pp. 38–39.

Inose, Hiroshi, and John R. Pierce. *Information Technology and Civilization.* New York: W. H. Freeman, 1984.

McIntosh, David K. "Interactive Distance Learning Technologies," *EITV Journal* (Educational and Industrial Television) (August 1984): 47–48.

Mosco, Vincent. *Pushbutton Fantasies: Critical Perspectives on Videotex and Information Technology.* Norwoods, NY: Ablex Publishing Co., 1983.

Wicklein, John. *Electronic Nightmare: The Home Communications Set and Your Freedom.* Boston: Beacon Press, 1979.

Sigel, Efrem, ed. *Videotex: The Coming Revolution in Home/Office Information Retrieval.* New York: Crown Publishers, 1980.

St. Lawrence, Jim. "The Interactive Videodisk: Here at Last," *Electronic Learning* 3 (April 1984): 49–57.

Issues

Danzinger, J., W. H. Dutton, and R. Kling. *Computers and Politics.* New York: Columbia University Press, 1981.

Dizard, Wilson. *The Coming Information Age: An Overview of Technology, Economics, and Politics.* New York: Longman, 1982.

Isaacson, Portia. "The Personal Computer versus Personal Privacy." In *Computers and Privacy in the Next Decade,* edited by Lance J. Hoffman. New York: Academic Press, 1980.

Kling, R. "Computers and Social Power," *Computers and Society* 5 (1974): 6–11.

Laudon, Kenneth. *Communications Technology and Democratic Participation.* New York: Praeger, 1977.

Miller, Arthur. *The Assault on Privacy: Computers, Data Banks, and Dossiers.* Ann

Arbor: University of Michigan Press, 1971.
Pool, Ithiel de Sola. *Technologies of Freedom: On Free Speech in an Electronic Age.* Cambridge: Harvard University Press, 1983.
Privacy Protection Study Commission. *Personal Privacy in an Information Society.* Washington, D.C.: U.S. Government Printing Office, 1977.
Westin, Alan. *Privacy and Freedom.* New York: Atheneum, 1967.

☐   SECTION TWO: SOFTWARE FOR CLASSROOM APPLICATIONS   ☐

Drill and Practice and Tutorials

AFRICA (and several other titles). Educational Activities, Inc., P.O. Box 392, Freeport, NY 11520.
AMERICAN HISTORY ADVENTURE (also WORLD HISTORY ADVENTURE, WORLD GEOGRAPHY ADVENTURE). Intellectual Software, 798 North Ave., Bridgeport, CT 06606.
CAPITALS OF STATES. Minnesota Educational Computing Consortium (MECC), 3490 Lexington Ave. North, St. Paul, MN 55112; and several other suppliers (public domain).
THE DECADES GAME. Brain Bank Software, 220 Fifth Avenue, New York, NY 10001.
LAW IN AMERICAN HISTORY. Oronoque Computer Concepts, Inc., Williamstown, VT 05679.
SMALLTOWN USA. Island Software, Box 300, Lake Grove, NY 11755.
THE TIME TUNNEL SERIES (several titles). Focus Media, 839 Stewart Ave., Box 865, Garden City, NY 11530.
UNLOCKING THE MAP CODE. Rand McNally, P.O. Box 7600, Chicago, IL 60680.
U.S. CONSTITUTION TUTOR. Micro Lab, 2699 Skokie Valley Rd., Highland Park, IL 60035.

Simulations

ANNAM. Educational Activities, P.O. Box 392, Freeport, NY 11520.
CARTELS & CUTTHROATS. Opportunities for Learning, Inc., 8950 Lurline Ave., Chatsworth, CA 91311.
GEOGRAPHY SEARCH (also COMMUNITY SEARCH, ARCHAEOLOGY SEARCH). McGraw-Hill Software, 1221 Avenue of the Americas, New York, NY 10020.
HOW A BILL BECOMES LAW. Intellectual Software, 798 North Ave., Bridgeport, CT 06606.
JENNY OF THE PRAIRIE. Rhiannon Software, Addison-Wesley Publishing Co., Reading, MA 01867.
THE HOUSE THAT JILL BUILT. CBS Software, 383 Madison Ave., New York, NY 10017.
MARBURY v. MADISON (Law in American History Series 2). Oronoque Computer Concepts, Inc., Williamstown, VT 05679.
OREGON TRAIL. Minnesota Educational Computing Consortium (MECC), 3490 Lexington Ave. North, St. Paul, MN 55112.

PRESIDENT ELECT. Strategic Simulations, Inc., 465 Fairchild Dr., Suite 108, Mountain View, CA 94043.

On-site Data Bases

DATABASE, JR. Oronoque Computer Concepts, Inc., Williamstown, VT 05679.

DEMOCOMP SERIES (maps and graphs: United States, Asia, and Africa series). Focus Media, 839 Stewart Ave., Box 865, Garden City, NY 11530.

PFS:FILE. Software Publishing Corp., 1901 Landings Drive, Mountain View, CA 94043.

POLLS AND POLITICS. Minnesota Educational Computing Consortium (MECC), 3490 Lexington Ave. North, St. Paul, MN 55112.

SUPERMAP. Sonoma Softworks, 10260 Bradley Ave., Cupertino, CA 95104.

USA DISPLAY. Instant Recall, P.O. Box 30134, Bethesda, MD 20814.

U.S. HISTORY DATA FILES (also U.S. GOVERNMENT DATA FILES; usable with PFS:FILE data base program). Scholastic Software, Scholastic Inc., 730 Broadway, New York, NY 10003.

Off-site Data Bases and Communications Networks

BRS (Bibliographic Retrieval Services), 1200 Route 7, Latham, NY 12110. Tel: (800) 883-4707.

CompuServe, 5000 Arlington Centre Blvd., Box 20212, Columbus, OH 43320. Tel: (800) 848-8990.

DIALOG Information Services, 3460 Hillview Ave., Palo Alto, CA 94304. Tel: (800) 227-1927.

Dow Jones News/Retrieval Service, P.O. Box 300, Princeton, NJ 08540. Tel: (609) 452-2000.

Times-On-Line Services, Inc., 1719A, Route 10, Parsippany, NJ 07054. Tel: (201) 267-2268.

ORBIT Information Retrieval System, 2500 Colorado Ave., Santa Monica, CA 90406. Tel: (800) 421-7229.

The Source, 1616 Anderson Road, McLean, VA 22102. Tel: (800) 336-3330.

Word Processing

APPLE WRITER. Apple Computer Corp., 20525 Mariani Ave., Cupertino, CA 95014.

APPLEWORKS. Apple Computer Corp., 20525 Mariani Ave., Cupertino, CA 95014.

BANK STREET WRITER. Available from Broderbund Software, 1938 Fourth Street, San Rafael, CA, 94901; or Scholastic, Inc., 730 Broadway, New York, NY 10003.

EASY SCRIPT. Commodore Computer Co., 487 Devon Park Drive, Wayne, PA 19087.

HOMEWORD. Sierra On-Line, Inc., Sierra On-Line Building, Coarsegold, CA 93614.

SCRIPSIT. Tandy Center/Radio Shack Corp., Computer Customer Service, Dept. 7879, Fort Worth, TX 76102.

WORDSTAR. MicroPro International, 33 San Pablo Ave., San Rafael, CA 94903.

Graphics and Statistics

LOTUS 1-2-3. Lotus Development Corp., 161 First St., Cambridge, MA 02142.
SPREADSHEET, JR. and DATABASE, JR. Oronoque Computer Concepts, Williamstown, VT 05679.
PFS:GRAPH. Software Publishing Corp., 1901 Landings Drive, Mountain View, CA 94043.
VISICALC. VisiCorp and Software Arts, Inc., 2895 Zanker Rd., San Jose, CA 95134.

Authoring Systems

APPLE PILOT. Apple Computer Corp., 20525 Mariani Ave., Cupertino, CA 95014.
THE ADAPTABLE SKELETON. Micro Power and Light, 12820 Hillcrest Rd. #224, Dallas, TX 75230.
THE LEARNING SYSTEM. Micro Lab, 2699 Skokie Valley Rd., Highland Park, IL 60035.
McGRAW-HILL AUTHORING SYSTEM. McGraw-Hill Software, 1221 Avenue of the Americas, New York, NY 10020.
TEST WRITER. Persimmon Software, 502 S. Savannah St., Greensboro, NC 27406.
TUTORIAL QUIZ MASTER. Random House, 400 Hahn Rd., Westminster, MD 21157.

Administration and Classroom Management

COMPUTERIZED GRADEBOOK. Electronic Coursework Systems, P.O. Box 2374-Station A, Champaign, IL 61820.
ELECTRONIC GRADEBOOK. Intellectual Software, 798 North Ave., Bridgeport, CT 06606.
GRADE AVERAGES. Educational Activities, P.O. Box 392, Freeport, NY 11520.
OMEGA LEARN. Omega Learning Systems, 5275 Edina Industrial Blvd., Edina, MN 55435.
THE SCHOOL TOOL. Brittanica Corp., 425 Michigan Ave., Chicago, IL 60611.
STUDENT DATA BASE. Intellectual Software, 798 North Ave., Bridgeport, CT 06606.

Index

American Association of University Women, 92–93
American Women in Science, 92
Apple Computer Company, 41, 45
Apple computers, 62, 75
APPLE WRITER, 55, 56
Association for Women in Computing, 93
Audiotapes, cassette, 81–82
Authoring languages, 31, 75–76
Authoring systems, 75–76

BANK STREET WRITER, 55–56
BASIC, 15, 75
Bibliographic Retrieval Systems (BRS), 48, 52
Billboards, computerized, 85
Books, irreplaceability of, 5
Bytes, 40

CAPITALS OF STATES, 25–26, 29
Card readers, 79, 80
Central Processing Unit (CPU), 13, 14, 19
Chips, 13
Classroom management programs, 70–74
Commodore computers, 62
CompuServe, 48, 49–51, 52, 84
Computer Assisted Instruction (CAI) programs, 21–40
Computers. *See also* Microcomputers
  business decisions made by, 103
  classroom introduction of, 10–11
  classroom management and, 8, 37, 70–74
  compatibility of, 85
  coping with, 9–10
  devices interfaced with, 77–89
  equity in access to, 10, 90–96
  in future societies, 9, 88–89, 91
  graphic capabilities of, 9, 26, 30, 58, 62–70

  human qualities reflected by, 5
  interactive capabilities of, 6, 8
  job opportunities in, 93
  job preparation and, 9, 102
  labor safety and, 102–103
  mainframe, 14–15, 85
  networking of, 15, 28, 85
  in photography, 99
  pirating information with, 98
  "sensory systems" of, 87
  social skills enhanced by, 38–39
  socioeconomic differences and, 93–94
  speed of, 19, 40
  students' access to, 30–31, 35
  teachers' access to, 6, 30
  teachers' fears of, 6–7, 33, 39
  teachers' irreplaceability by, 5, 56
  women and, 91–93
  worldwide use of, 94

Data, 40
  potential misuses of, 41, 97–98
DATABASE, JR., 66–70
Data base programs, 9, 22
  classroom uses of, 42–43, 45–47
  costs of, 48, 49, 54
  disadvantages of, 54
  educational value of, 40–41, 47–48
  future of, 70
  logistical problems of, 48–49
  off-site, 41, 47–54, 77
  on-site, 41–47
  services for, 47–54
  with statistical and graphic capabilities, 66–70
  videotex systems as, 86–87
Data files, 18, 19
dBASE II, 70
DECADES GAME, 24–25
DEMOCOMP SERIES, 43

11

A 28 87 2